The Pulse of Power: Navigating Modern Politics and Society

Laurel D. Malvern

"The Pulse of Power: Navigating Modern Politics and Society"

Preface

In the early hours of a chilly morning in January 2024, I found myself reflecting on the profound changes our world has undergone in recent decades. The rapid evolution of technology, the shifting dynamics of global power, and the increasingly urgent cries for social justice have created a landscape that is both exhilarating and daunting. It was in this moment of contemplation that the idea for this book, "The Pulse of Power: Navigating Modern Politics and Society," was born.

The intent behind this book is to provide a comprehensive and accessible guide to the complex and often bewildering world of modern politics and society. We live in an era where the boundaries between local and global issues have blurred, where the personal is often political, and where understanding the intricate web of influences that shape our lives is more crucial than ever.

Throughout my career as a political analyst and educator, I have encountered countless individuals seeking clarity and insight into the forces that govern our world. Students, colleagues, and curious minds alike have expressed a desire to grasp the interconnectedness of political systems, social structures, economic policies, and global relations. This book aims to fulfill that desire, offering a holistic perspective that bridges the gaps between these vital areas of study.

"The Pulse of Power" is structured to take readers on a journey through the historical foundations of governance, the theoretical underpinnings of political thought, and the practical implications of economic and social policies. It delves into the cultural and societal factors that influence political behavior and examines the impact of globalization and international relations on domestic affairs. By the end of this journey, I hope readers will have a deeper appreciation for the complexity and interdependence of the world we inhabit.

Writing this book has been a labor of love, driven by a passion for understanding and explaining the multifaceted nature of our political and social environment. I am deeply indebted to the many scholars, activists, and practitioners whose work has informed and inspired my own. Their contributions have been invaluable in shaping the content and perspective of this book.

I also want to acknowledge the support of my family, friends, and colleagues, whose encouragement and feedback have been instrumental throughout this process. Their belief in the importance of this project has sustained me during the many months of research and writing.

As you embark on this exploration of modern politics and society, I encourage you to approach it with an open mind and a critical eye. The challenges we face are complex and multifaceted, but they are not insurmountable. By understanding the forces at play and engaging actively in the political process, each of us has the potential to contribute to a more just and equitable world.

Thank you for joining me on this journey. I hope "The Pulse of Power" will serve as a valuable resource and a source of inspiration as we navigate the ever-changing landscape of modern politics and society together.

Sincerely,

Laurel D. Malvern

Introduction: The Landscape of Modern Politics and Society

In the early 21st century, the world stands at a crossroads. Political landscapes are shifting, societies are evolving, and the forces that shape our daily lives are more interconnected than ever before. Understanding these dynamics is crucial for navigating the complexities of our time. This introduction sets the stage for a comprehensive exploration of modern politics and society, delving into the multifaceted relationships that define our global environment in 2024.

The Interconnectedness of Politics, Social Sciences, and Current Events

Politics today cannot be viewed in isolation. It intertwines with social sciences and current events, creating a web of influences that affect governance, policy-making, and public opinion. Social structures, economic conditions, cultural norms, and technological advancements all play pivotal roles in shaping political landscapes. For instance, the rise of social media has transformed political campaigning and public engagement, allowing for unprecedented levels of interaction between citizens and their leaders.

Moreover, global events such as climate change, pandemics, and international conflicts have local repercussions, influencing national policies and societal attitudes. Understanding these connections is essential for grasping the full picture of modern politics. This book aims to dissect these relationships, providing readers with a holistic view of how different factors interweave to shape our world.

The Importance of Understanding These Connections in 2024 As we navigate the complexities of 2024, the need for a nuanced understanding of politics and society has never been greater. The past few years have been marked by significant upheavals and transformations. From the COVID-19 pandemic that redefined public health policies and economic strategies, to the ongoing debates around social justice and inequality, each event has underscored the importance of informed political and social engagement.

In addition, technological innovations continue to accelerate, bringing both opportunities and challenges. Artificial intelligence, for example, is revolutionizing industries but also raising ethical and regulatory concerns. Similarly, the global push for sustainability and environmental protection is reshaping economic policies and international relations.

In this context, being well-informed is not just advantageous; it is imperative. Whether you are a student, a professional, or a curious citizen, understanding the intricate landscape of modern politics and society empowers you to make informed decisions, participate in meaningful discussions, and contribute to positive change.

What This Book Offers
"The Pulse of Power: Navigating Modern Politics and Society" is designed to be a comprehensive guide for anyone seeking to understand the current political and social climate. The book is divided into five parts, each focusing on different aspects of politics and society:

Foundations of Power and Governance: This section explores the historical evolution of political systems, major political theories, and the structure of governments. It lays the groundwork for understanding how past events and ideas influence present-day governance.

The Dynamics of Society and Culture: Here, we examine how societal structures and cultural norms impact political behavior. Topics include the role of social institutions, anthropological insights into political systems, and the influence of social movements and activism.

Economics and Public Policy: This part delves into the economic principles that drive political decisions and the crafting of public policies. It also addresses issues of inequality and social justice, highlighting policies and movements aimed at promoting equity.

Global Perspectives and International Relations: Understanding the global context is crucial in today's interconnected world. This section covers globalization, international diplomacy, and human rights, providing a broader perspective on how global events shape national politics.

Democracy in Action: The final section focuses on electoral politics, democratic engagement, and the role of activism in democratic societies. It offers practical insights into how citizens can participate in and influence the political process.

By the end of this journey, readers will have a deeper understanding of the interconnected forces that shape modern politics and society. This knowledge will equip them to navigate the complexities of our time with confidence and insight, contributing to a more informed and engaged citizenry.

Welcome to "The Pulse of Power: Navigating Modern Politics and Society." Let's embark on this enlightening journey together.

Chapter 1: Overview of the Interconnectedness of Politics, Social Sciences, and Current Events

In the contemporary world, politics, social sciences, and current events are deeply intertwined, creating a complex web that influences every aspect of our lives. This chapter provides an overview of this interconnectedness, exploring how political systems are shaped by social structures, cultural norms, economic conditions, and technological advancements. Understanding these connections is essential for grasping the nuances of modern governance and societal dynamics.

The Role of Social Sciences in Politics
Social sciences—including sociology, anthropology, economics, and psychology—play a crucial role in understanding political behavior and decision-making processes. These disciplines offer insights into how societal structures and cultural norms shape individual and collective actions, influencing everything from voting patterns to policy preferences.

Sociology examines how social institutions (e.g., family, education, religion) and group dynamics impact political behavior. For instance, sociological studies have shown that family background and educational attainment significantly influence political participation and ideological leanings.

Anthropology provides a deeper understanding of cultural influences on political systems. By studying different cultures, anthropologists reveal how traditions, beliefs, and values shape political norms and governance structures.

Economics analyzes how resource allocation, wealth distribution, and economic policies affect political stability and public policy. Economic conditions often drive political agendas, with issues like unemployment, inflation, and income inequality taking center stage in political debates.

Psychology helps explain the cognitive and emotional factors that influence political attitudes and behaviors. Understanding psychological drivers, such as fear, identity, and group loyalty, is essential for comprehending phenomena like political polarization and populism.

The Impact of Current Events on Politics and Society Current events, from global crises to local incidents, have immediate and far-reaching impacts on politics and society. These events can shift public opinion, alter political priorities, and trigger social movements.

Global Crises: Events like the COVID-19 pandemic highlight the interconnectedness of health, economics, and politics. The pandemic not only strained healthcare systems but also led to economic downturns and influenced political discourse around public health policies, economic relief measures, and government accountability.

Environmental Challenges: Climate change and environmental degradation are pressing issues that cross national borders, affecting international relations and domestic policies. Environmental policies, debates over renewable energy, and international agreements like the Paris Agreement illustrate the global nature of these challenges.

Technological Advancements: The rapid pace of technological innovation impacts politics and society in profound ways. Social media, for example, has revolutionized political campaigning, enabling instant communication and mobilization but also raising concerns about misinformation and digital privacy.

Social Movements: Movements advocating for social justice, such as Black Lives Matter and #MeToo, have brought issues of racial and gender equality to the forefront of political discourse. These movements demonstrate the power of grassroots activism in influencing public opinion and policy changes.

The Dynamic Interplay of Politics, Social Sciences, and Current Events
The interplay between politics, social sciences, and current events creates a dynamic environment where each element influences and is influenced by the others.

Policy Formation: Social science research informs policymakers about the potential impacts of their decisions. For example, economic models can predict the effects of tax reforms, while sociological studies can guide policies on education and healthcare.

Public Opinion: Current events shape public opinion, which in turn influences political agendas. Politicians often respond to the concerns raised by significant events, whether it's a natural disaster, economic crisis, or social upheaval.

Cultural Shifts: Changes in societal values and cultural norms can lead to significant political transformations. For instance, the growing acceptance of LGBTQ+ rights has led to policy changes and legal reforms in many countries.

Globalization: The interconnectedness of the global economy means that political decisions in one country can have ripple effects worldwide. Trade agreements, international conflicts, and global health issues exemplify how local politics are influenced by and contribute to global trends.

Conclusion
Understanding the interconnectedness of politics, social sciences, and current events is essential for navigating the complexities of our modern world. This chapter has provided an overview of how these elements interact and influence each other, setting the stage for a deeper exploration of the themes that will be covered in this book. As we move forward, we will delve into the historical foundations, theoretical frameworks, and practical implications of these interconnected forces, equipping readers with the knowledge to make informed decisions and engage meaningfully in political and social discourse.

By recognizing the intricate web of influences that shape our world, we can better understand the challenges we face and work towards creating a more informed, equitable, and just society.

Chapter 2: The Importance of Understanding These Connections in 2024

As we navigate the complexities of 2024, the interconnectedness of politics, social sciences, and current events becomes increasingly critical. This chapter explores why understanding these connections is essential for making informed decisions, engaging in meaningful discussions, and contributing to positive societal change in today's rapidly evolving world.

The Rapid Pace of Technological Advancement Technological innovation continues to accelerate, transforming every aspect of our lives, including politics and society. Advances in artificial intelligence, big data, and social media have reshaped how political campaigns are conducted, how information is disseminated, and how public opinion is formed.

Artificial Intelligence and Big Data: AI and big data analytics provide powerful tools for political campaigns, enabling more precise targeting of voters and personalized communication strategies. However, these technologies also raise ethical and privacy concerns, making it essential to understand their implications for democracy and individual rights.

Social Media and Information Dissemination: Social media platforms have become primary sources of news and information, but they also facilitate the spread of misinformation and fake news. Understanding the dynamics of social media is crucial for navigating the modern information landscape and safeguarding the integrity of democratic processes.

The Global Impact of Economic Policies
Economic conditions and policies have far-reaching effects on both national and global scales. In 2024, the world faces numerous economic challenges, from recovery post-pandemic to addressing income inequality and fostering sustainable development.

Economic Recovery Post-Pandemic: The economic fallout from the COVID-19 pandemic continues to shape policy decisions worldwide. Understanding economic principles and the impact of fiscal and monetary policies is vital for assessing government responses and advocating for effective solutions.

Income Inequality: Growing disparities in wealth and income pose significant challenges to social cohesion and political stability. An informed perspective on economic inequality can guide discussions on policies aimed at promoting social justice and equitable growth.

Sustainable Development: The push for sustainability and environmental protection influences economic policies globally. Recognizing the interconnectedness of economic growth, environmental health, and social well-being is crucial for supporting policies that balance these priorities.

The Evolving Nature of Social Movements

Social movements play a pivotal role in shaping political discourse and driving policy changes. In 2024, movements advocating for social justice, climate action, and human rights continue to gain momentum, demonstrating the power of collective action.

Social Justice Movements: Movements like Black Lives Matter and #MeToo have brought issues of racial and gender inequality to the forefront. Understanding the history and dynamics of these movements is essential for engaging in informed advocacy and supporting meaningful reforms.

Climate Action: Climate change activism has spurred significant policy initiatives aimed at reducing carbon emissions and promoting sustainability. Recognizing the scientific, economic, and political dimensions of climate action is critical for supporting effective environmental policies.

Human Rights Advocacy: Global efforts to protect human rights are influenced by cultural, political, and economic factors. An informed understanding of these issues helps promote policies that uphold human dignity and justice worldwide.

The Influence of Globalization
Globalization continues to shape politics, economics, and society in profound ways. In 2024, the interconnectedness of the global economy, international relations, and cultural exchanges underscores the importance of understanding global dynamics.

International Relations: Diplomatic relations, trade agreements, and international conflicts have significant implications for national policies and global stability. Understanding the principles of international relations helps navigate the complexities of global politics and advocate for peaceful cooperation.

Global Economy: The interconnected global economy means that economic policies in one country can have ripple effects worldwide. Recognizing the impact of globalization on economic conditions and labor markets is essential for supporting policies that foster global prosperity and fairness.

Cultural Exchanges: The exchange of ideas, values, and traditions across borders enriches societies but also presents challenges related to cultural identity and integration. Understanding the benefits and challenges of cultural globalization helps promote inclusive and harmonious societies.

The Role of Education and Civic Engagement
Informed and active citizens are the cornerstone of a healthy democracy. In 2024, fostering education and civic engagement is more important than ever for addressing the complex challenges facing our world.

Education: Comprehensive education that encompasses political science, economics, and social studies equips individuals with the knowledge to understand and navigate contemporary issues. Promoting education in these areas is vital for developing critical thinking and informed decision-making.

Civic Engagement: Active participation in the political process, from voting to advocacy, is essential for a functioning democracy. Understanding the mechanisms of civic engagement and the importance of activism empowers individuals to contribute to positive societal change.

Media Literacy: In an era of information overload, media literacy is crucial for discerning credible sources and navigating the digital landscape. Educating individuals on how to critically evaluate information supports informed and responsible civic participation.

Conclusion
In 2024, the interconnectedness of politics, social sciences, and current events demands our attention and understanding. By comprehending these connections, we are better equipped to navigate the complexities of our time, make informed decisions, and contribute to a more just and equitable society. This chapter has highlighted the importance of this interconnectedness, setting the stage for a deeper exploration of the themes that will be covered in this book. As we move forward, we will delve into the historical foundations, theoretical frameworks, and practical implications of these interconnected forces, providing readers with the knowledge and tools to engage meaningfully in the political and social landscape of today.

Chapter 3: Foundations of Power and Governance

Understanding the foundations of power and governance is crucial for comprehending the complexities of modern political systems. This chapter delves into the historical evolution of governance, key political theories, and the structure of government, providing a comprehensive background to better understand contemporary political landscapes.

Historical Evolution of Political Systems
The history of political systems is marked by significant milestones that have shaped the governance structures we see today. These systems have evolved over centuries, influenced by cultural, economic, and social factors.

Ancient Civilizations:

Mesopotamia and Egypt: Early forms of centralized authority emerged in ancient Mesopotamia and Egypt, where rulers wielded absolute power often justified by divine right.
Greece and Rome: Ancient Greece introduced the concept of democracy, particularly in Athens, where citizens participated directly in decision-making. The Roman Republic, with its Senate and consuls, contributed to the development of representative government structures.

Feudalism and Monarchy:

Medieval Europe: The collapse of the Roman Empire led to the rise of feudalism, a decentralized system where local lords held power over their lands and owed allegiance to a monarch. This period also saw the growth of the church's influence over political matters.
Absolute Monarchies: By the early modern period, many European states transitioned to absolute monarchies, where kings and queens held unparalleled power, often justified by the notion of divine right.
Enlightenment and Revolution:

The Enlightenment: Enlightenment thinkers such as John Locke, Jean-Jacques Rousseau, and Montesquieu challenged absolute authority and advocated for individual rights, separation of powers, and social contracts.
Revolutions: The American and French Revolutions in the late 18th century were pivotal, establishing republics based on principles of liberty, equality, and fraternity, and significantly influencing subsequent democratic movements worldwide.
Modern Political Systems:

Constitutional Democracies: The 19th and 20th centuries saw the rise of constitutional democracies, where the rule of law and individual rights were enshrined in constitutions.
Totalitarian Regimes: The 20th century also witnessed the emergence of totalitarian regimes, such as Nazi Germany and the Soviet Union, characterized by centralized control and suppression of dissent.
Post-Colonial States: The decolonization process post-World War II led to the creation of new states with diverse political systems, often blending traditional governance structures with modern principles.
Major Political Theories and Thinkers

Political theories provide frameworks for understanding how power and governance should be structured and exercised. Key political thinkers have shaped these theories, offering diverse perspectives on governance.

Classical Political Theory:

Plato and Aristotle: Plato's vision of a philosopher-king and Aristotle's classification of government types (monarchy, aristocracy, and polity) laid foundational ideas for political thought.
Social Contract Theory:

Thomas Hobbes: In "Leviathan," Hobbes argued that a strong central authority is necessary to avoid the chaos of the state of nature.
John Locke: Locke's "Two Treatises of Government" emphasized natural rights and the idea that government's legitimacy comes from the consent of the governed.
Jean-Jacques Rousseau: Rousseau's "The Social Contract" introduced the concept of general will and popular sovereignty.
Liberalism and Conservatism:

John Stuart Mill: Mill's advocacy for individual liberty and representative democracy in "On Liberty" and "Considerations on Representative Government" influenced liberal thought.
Edmund Burke: Burke's emphasis on tradition, social order, and gradual change in "Reflections on the Revolution in France" laid the groundwork for modern conservatism.
Marxism and Socialism:

Karl Marx and Friedrich Engels: In "The Communist Manifesto," Marx and Engels critiqued capitalism and advocated for a classless society through the abolition of private property and the means of production.

Social Democracy: Evolving from Marxist thought, social democracy advocates for a balance between market economy and social welfare, emphasizing state intervention to promote social justice.

Modern Political Theory:

Hannah Arendt: Arendt's analysis of totalitarianism and her exploration of power, authority, and democracy in works like "The Origins of Totalitarianism" remain influential.

John Rawls: Rawls' "A Theory of Justice" introduced the idea of justice as fairness and the concept of the original position and the veil of ignorance.

The Structure of Government

Understanding the structure of government is essential for analyzing how power is distributed and exercised within a state. Different systems of government have distinct features and functions.

Types of Government Systems:

Democracy: In democratic systems, power is vested in the people, who exercise it directly or through elected representatives. Key features include free and fair elections, protection of individual rights, and the rule of law.

Autocracy: Autocratic systems concentrate power in the hands of a single ruler or a small group, often characterized by limited political pluralism and individual freedoms.

Oligarchy: In oligarchies, power resides with a small, elite group based on wealth, family ties, or military control.

Theocracy: Theocracies are governed by religious leaders or according to religious laws, where political authority is often intertwined with religious authority.

Branches of Government:

Executive: The executive branch, headed by the president or prime minister, is responsible for implementing laws and running the day-to-day affairs of the government.
Legislative: The legislative branch, composed of elected representatives, is responsible for making laws. It can be unicameral (single chamber) or bicameral (two chambers, such as a senate and house of representatives).
Judicial: The judicial branch interprets laws and ensures they are applied fairly. It acts as a check on the executive and legislative branches by upholding constitutional principles and individual rights.
Federal and Unitary Systems:

Federal Systems: In federal systems, power is divided between a central government and regional governments (states or provinces), allowing for a balance of power and local autonomy.
Unitary Systems: Unitary systems concentrate power in a central government, with regional authorities having limited autonomy and mainly implementing central directives.
Conclusion
The foundations of power and governance provide a crucial backdrop for understanding contemporary political systems. By exploring the historical evolution of governance, key political theories, and the structure of government, we gain insights into the forces that shape our political landscapes. This knowledge equips us to engage more effectively with the complexities of modern politics and contribute to informed discourse and decision-making. As we move forward, this foundational understanding will serve as a basis for examining the dynamics of society, economics, and international relations in subsequent chapters.

Chapter 4: A Historical Perspective on Government and Politics

To truly understand the contemporary political landscape, it's essential to delve into the historical development of government and politics. This chapter explores key milestones in the evolution of political systems, tracing how governance structures have transformed over time and how these changes have shaped modern politics.

Ancient Political Systems
Mesopotamia and Egypt: The Birth of Centralized Authority

Mesopotamia: As one of the earliest civilizations, Mesopotamia saw the emergence of city-states governed by kings who combined religious and political authority. The Code of Hammurabi exemplifies early legal systems that governed society.
Egypt: Pharaohs in ancient Egypt wielded absolute power, seen as divine rulers. This theocratic governance integrated religious beliefs with political authority, laying the groundwork for future centralized states.
Greece and Rome: Foundations of Democracy and Republic

Ancient Greece: Particularly in Athens, democracy flourished with citizens participating directly in decision-making processes. Concepts like citizenship, political equality, and public debate were pioneered here.

Roman Republic: The Roman Republic introduced a mixed system with elements of democracy (popular assemblies) and oligarchy (Senate). The Republic's system of checks and balances influenced many modern democratic structures.

Medieval and Renaissance Political Thought

Feudalism: Decentralized Power Structures

Medieval Europe: Following the fall of the Roman Empire, Europe fragmented into numerous feudal states. Local lords held power, owing allegiance to monarchs, but with significant autonomy. This period saw the rise of a hierarchical system based on land ownership and vassalage.

The Rise of Monarchies:

Absolute Monarchies: By the late Middle Ages, many European countries saw the consolidation of power in the hands of monarchs. The concept of divine right justified absolute rule, as seen in the reigns of Louis XIV of France and the Tudors in England.

The Renaissance and Early Modern Thought:

Machiavelli: In "The Prince," Niccolò Machiavelli offered pragmatic advice on political leadership, emphasizing realpolitik and the effective exercise of power, often devoid of moral considerations.

The Enlightenment: Philosophers like John Locke, Jean-Jacques Rousseau, and Montesquieu challenged absolute authority, advocating for natural rights, social contracts, and the separation of powers. Their ideas laid the intellectual groundwork for modern democratic thought.

Revolutionary Changes

The American Revolution: Birth of a New Nation

Independence and Constitution: The American Revolution (1775-1783) marked a significant shift towards self-governance and republicanism. The U.S. Constitution established a federal system with a clear separation of powers, checks and balances, and a Bill of Rights ensuring individual liberties.
The French Revolution: Radical Transformation

Liberty, Equality, Fraternity: The French Revolution (1789-1799) dismantled the absolute monarchy and aristocratic privileges, leading to the rise of the French Republic. It introduced radical ideas about citizenship, secularism, and human rights, influencing revolutionary movements across the globe.
19th and 20th Century Developments
Industrialization and Political Change:

Economic Shifts: The Industrial Revolution brought profound economic and social changes, leading to the rise of new political ideologies such as socialism and communism. Karl Marx and Friedrich Engels critiqued the capitalist system and proposed a revolutionary path towards a classless society.
Labor Movements: The growth of industrial labor led to organized movements demanding better working conditions, wages, and rights, significantly influencing political policies and party formations.
Imperialism and Nationalism:

Colonial Empires: The 19th century was marked by the expansion of European empires. The political control over colonies and the exploitation of resources had long-lasting impacts on global politics and economics.

Nationalist Movements: Nationalism emerged as a powerful force, uniting people based on shared identity and leading to the formation of nation-states. The unifications of Germany and Italy are prime examples of nationalist-driven political change.
The World Wars and Their Aftermath:

World War I and II: The two world wars dramatically altered the political landscape, leading to the collapse of empires and the rise of new superpowers. The interwar period saw the rise of totalitarian regimes, while the post-World War II era marked the beginning of the Cold War and the decolonization process.
The United Nations: Established in 1945, the UN aimed to prevent future conflicts and promote international cooperation. Its formation marked a shift towards multilateralism and collective security in global politics.
Cold War Era: Ideological Confrontation:

Capitalism vs. Communism: The Cold War (1947-1991) was characterized by the ideological struggle between the capitalist United States and the communist Soviet Union. This period saw the proliferation of nuclear weapons, proxy wars, and the division of the world into spheres of influence.
Decolonization: The mid-20th century witnessed the end of colonial rule in Asia, Africa, and the Caribbean, leading to the emergence of newly independent states with diverse political systems.
Contemporary Political Systems
Post-Cold War and Globalization:

End of the Cold War: The dissolution of the Soviet Union in 1991 marked the end of the Cold War, leading to the spread of liberal democracy and market economies. However, this period also saw the rise of ethnic conflicts and regional instability.

Globalization: The late 20th and early 21st centuries have been characterized by increased global interconnectedness. Economic globalization, technological advancements, and cultural exchanges have reshaped political dynamics, leading to both opportunities and challenges.
21st Century Challenges:

Terrorism and Security: The 9/11 attacks in 2001 highlighted the threat of global terrorism, leading to significant changes in international security policies and the rise of surveillance states.
Climate Change: Environmental issues have become central to global politics, with international agreements like the Paris Accord aiming to address climate change and promote sustainable development.
Populism and Political Polarization: Recent years have seen a rise in populist movements challenging established political norms and institutions, leading to increased political polarization and debates over the future of democracy.
Conclusion
The historical evolution of government and politics is a testament to humanity's ongoing quest for better governance, justice, and societal well-being. From ancient city-states to modern democracies, political systems have continually adapted to changing social, economic, and cultural contexts. By understanding this historical trajectory, we can better appreciate the complexities of contemporary political structures and the enduring challenges of governance. As we move forward in this book, this historical perspective will provide a foundation for exploring the dynamic interplay between politics, society, and current events in the modern world.

Chapter 5: Evolution of Political Systems

The evolution of political systems reflects the dynamic interplay between societal needs, cultural values, and historical circumstances. This chapter traces the development of political systems from ancient civilizations to modern democracies, exploring how governance structures have evolved over time and the enduring influences that shape contemporary politics.

Ancient and Classical Political Systems
Mesopotamia and Egypt: Early Forms of Governance

Mesopotamia: Among the earliest civilizations, Mesopotamia developed city-states governed by monarchs who claimed divine authority. The Code of Hammurabi (c. 1754 BCE) established one of the earliest known legal codes, illustrating early efforts to codify governance.
Egypt: Pharaohs in ancient Egypt ruled as divine monarchs, centralizing authority and administering vast bureaucratic systems that governed agriculture, trade, and religious affairs.
Ancient Greece: Birth of Democracy

Athens: Ancient Greece pioneered democratic governance in the city-state of Athens, where citizens participated directly in decision-making through assemblies and juries. Concepts like citizenship, equality before the law, and public debate laid the foundation for democratic principles.
Roman Republic: Republican Governance

Roman Senate: The Roman Republic (509-27 BCE) established a representative system where elected officials, such as consuls and senators, governed in the interests of the people. The Senate served as a deliberative body, balancing power among different classes and regions.
Feudalism and Monarchical Systems
Medieval Feudalism: Decentralized Power

Feudal System: Following the fall of the Roman Empire, feudalism emerged in medieval Europe, characterized by decentralized authority where local lords held power over their domains. Vassalage and feudal obligations structured societal relationships.
Rise of Monarchies: Centralization of Power

Absolute Monarchies: By the late Middle Ages, absolute monarchies consolidated power in the hands of kings and queens who claimed divine right to rule. Centralized bureaucracies and standing armies strengthened royal authority.
Early Modern and Enlightenment Thought
Early Modern Political Thought: Social Contract and Natural Rights

Thomas Hobbes: In "Leviathan" (1651), Hobbes argued for a social contract where individuals consented to a powerful sovereign to maintain order and prevent chaos.

John Locke: Locke's "Two Treatises of Government" (1689) articulated natural rights to life, liberty, and property, proposing that governments derive legitimacy from the consent of the governed.

Montesquieu: In "The Spirit of the Laws" (1748), Montesquieu advocated for separation of powers within government—legislative, executive, and judicial—ensuring checks and balances to prevent tyranny.

The Enlightenment: Democracy and Rational Governance

Jean-Jacques Rousseau: Rousseau's "The Social Contract" (1762) emphasized the general will and popular sovereignty, arguing for direct democracy and civic engagement.

Voltaire: Voltaire championed freedom of speech, religious tolerance, and separation of church and state, advocating for enlightened despotism.

19th and 20th Century Political Transformations

Industrialization and Social Movements

Industrial Revolution: Economic changes brought about by industrialization led to social upheaval and the rise of labor movements advocating for workers' rights, fair wages, and better working conditions.

Socialism and Marxism: Karl Marx and Friedrich Engels critiqued capitalism in "The Communist Manifesto" (1848), proposing a classless society where workers control the means of production.

Democracy and Nationalism

Democratic Revolutions: The American Revolution (1775-1783) and the French Revolution (1789-1799) established republics based on principles of liberty, equality, and fraternity, influencing global democratic movements.

Nationalism: Nationalist movements in the 19th century sought self-determination and independence from imperial rule, reshaping political boundaries and identities.

20th Century: World Wars and Ideological Struggles

Totalitarianism: Totalitarian regimes like Nazi Germany and Soviet Russia emerged, characterized by single-party rule, censorship, and state control over all aspects of life.
Cold War: The ideological confrontation between capitalism and communism defined global politics, leading to proxy wars, nuclear arms races, and geopolitical divisions.
Contemporary Political Systems and Global Challenges
Modern Democracies and Authoritarianism

Democratic Governance: Today, most Western countries embrace representative democracies with regular elections, civil liberties, and rule of law.
Authoritarianism: Authoritarian regimes in various parts of the world centralize power, restrict political freedoms, and suppress dissent.
Globalization and Multilateralism

Global Interdependence: Economic globalization, technological advancements, and cultural exchanges have interconnected nations, influencing international relations and governance.
Multilateral Organizations: Institutions like the United Nations promote cooperation on global issues such as climate change, human rights, and security.
Conclusion

The evolution of political systems reflects humanity's quest for governance structures that balance power, uphold rights, and foster societal well-being. From ancient civilizations to modern democracies, political systems have adapted to changing contexts, ideologies, and challenges. By examining this historical journey, we gain insights into the enduring influences that shape contemporary politics and the ongoing debates over governance, justice, and democracy. As we explore further in this book, understanding the evolution of political systems provides a foundation for analyzing current political dynamics and envisioning future possibilities in a globalized world.

Chapter 6: Key Historical Milestones Shaping Modern Governance

Modern governance is the product of centuries of historical developments, conflicts, and transformative ideas. This chapter examines pivotal historical milestones that have shaped the evolution of governance structures worldwide, influencing the principles, institutions, and practices of contemporary political systems.

Magna Carta (1215)

The Magna Carta, signed by King John of England in 1215, is a foundational document in the history of constitutional law and governance. It limited the monarch's powers by asserting the rights of nobles and establishing principles of due process and the rule of law. Although initially a document for the aristocracy, it later became a symbol of individual liberties and constraints on arbitrary authority, influencing subsequent constitutional developments.

The Enlightenment and Liberalism
The Enlightenment, a philosophical movement in 18th-century Europe, promoted rational thinking, individualism, and the questioning of traditional authority. It significantly influenced modern governance through the development of liberal ideas:

John Locke's Two Treatises of Government (1689): Locke argued for natural rights (life, liberty, and property) and the social contract theory, asserting that governments derive their legitimacy from the consent of the governed. His ideas laid the groundwork for constitutional democracy and limited government.

Montesquieu's The Spirit of the Laws (1748): Montesquieu advocated for the separation of powers within government — legislative, executive, and judicial — to prevent tyranny and ensure checks and balances. His ideas shaped the structures of modern democracies.

American Revolution (1775-1783) and Declaration of Independence (1776)

The American Revolution against British colonial rule resulted in the establishment of the United States as a republic based on democratic principles. The Declaration of Independence, authored by Thomas Jefferson, proclaimed universal principles of human rights, including the right to life, liberty, and the pursuit of happiness. It inspired revolutions and independence movements globally and influenced the development of constitutional democracies.

French Revolution (1789-1799) and Declaration of the Rights of Man and of the Citizen
The French Revolution marked a turning point in modern governance by overthrowing the absolute monarchy and promoting principles of popular sovereignty, equality before the law, and individual rights. The Declaration of the Rights of Man and of the Citizen (1789) asserted natural and civil rights, challenging traditional hierarchies and inspiring democratic movements worldwide.

Industrial Revolution and Social Movements
The Industrial Revolution in the 19th century brought profound economic and social changes, leading to the rise of labor movements and demands for political reforms:

Socialism and Marxism: Karl Marx and Friedrich Engels critiqued capitalist exploitation in "The Communist Manifesto" (1848), advocating for worker solidarity, class struggle, and the eventual establishment of a classless society. Marxist ideas influenced socialist movements and the development of welfare states.

Labor Movements: Workers organized labor unions and strikes to demand better working conditions, fair wages, and social protections. These movements pressured governments to enact labor laws and social reforms, shaping modern welfare policies.

World Wars and Global Governance
The 20th century was marked by two devastating world wars that reshaped global politics and governance:

League of Nations (1920) and United Nations (1945): The League of Nations, established after World War I, aimed to promote international cooperation and prevent future conflicts. Although it faced challenges and ultimately failed to prevent World War II, it laid the groundwork for the United Nations. The UN, founded in 1945 after World War II, seeks to maintain international peace and security, promote human rights, and foster global cooperation through its specialized agencies and peacekeeping missions.
Decolonization and the Rise of Nation-States
The mid-20th century witnessed the decolonization movements in Africa, Asia, and the Americas, leading to the establishment of new nation-states and the assertion of self-determination:

End of Colonial Empires: Colonized peoples fought for independence from European imperial powers, asserting their cultural, political, and economic sovereignty. The decolonization process reshaped global power dynamics and contributed to the development of international norms on self-determination and human rights.
Cold War and Political Ideologies
The Cold War rivalry between the United States and the Soviet Union shaped global politics and governance structures:

Capitalism vs. Communism: The ideological confrontation between capitalism and communism influenced political developments, alliances, and conflicts worldwide. The Cold War era saw the division of Europe into Eastern Bloc and Western Bloc countries and the proliferation of proxy wars.

Conclusion
The historical milestones outlined in this chapter have profoundly influenced the evolution of governance structures, principles, and practices in modern societies. From the Magna Carta to the United Nations, these pivotal moments reflect humanity's quest for political freedom, equality, and justice. Understanding these historical developments provides insights into contemporary political challenges and opportunities, guiding discussions on governance reforms, democratic principles, and global cooperation in the 21st century. As we explore further in this book, these milestones serve as crucial touchstones for examining the complex interplay between history, politics, and governance in shaping our world today.

Chapter 7: Political Theory and Its Modern Applications

Political theory provides a conceptual framework for understanding governance, power dynamics, and societal organization. This chapter explores major political theories and their contemporary applications, examining how theoretical insights shape modern political systems and policies.

Classical Political Theory
Plato's Republic and Aristotle's Politics

Plato: In "The Republic," Plato explores the ideal city-state governed by philosopher-kings, emphasizing justice, hierarchy, and the role of education in shaping virtuous leaders.

Aristotle: Aristotle's "Politics" examines different forms of government (monarchy, aristocracy, democracy) and their virtues and vices. He advocates for a mixed form of government that balances the interests of different social classes.

Social Contract Theory

Thomas Hobbes

Key Ideas: Hobbes, in "Leviathan," argues that humans in a state of nature are driven by self-interest and conflict. To avoid chaos, individuals form a social contract, surrendering some freedoms to a sovereign authority for mutual protection and security.

John Locke

Natural Rights: Locke's "Two Treatises of Government" asserts natural rights (life, liberty, property) and the right of rebellion against tyrannical rule. He proposes a social contract based on consent, with government's legitimacy derived from the people.

Jean-Jacques Rousseau

General Will: Rousseau's "The Social Contract" posits the concept of the general will, representing the common interests of citizens. He advocates for direct democracy where laws reflect the collective decision-making of the people.

Liberalism and Individualism

John Stuart Mill

On Liberty: Mill argues for individual liberty as essential for personal development and societal progress. He defends freedom of thought, expression, and action, while advocating for limits on state interference to prevent harm to others.
Isaiah Berlin

Two Concepts of Liberty: Berlin distinguishes between negative liberty (freedom from external constraints) and positive liberty (ability to achieve one's potential). He critiques authoritarianism and defends pluralism and individual choice.
Marxist and Critical Theories
Karl Marx

Historical Materialism: Marx's critique of capitalism in "Das Kapital" focuses on class struggle and the exploitation of labor. He predicts the eventual collapse of capitalism and the establishment of a classless society based on common ownership.
Antonio Gramsci

Hegemony and Cultural Marxism: Gramsci's concept of hegemony explores how ruling elites maintain dominance through cultural institutions and ideology. He emphasizes the role of intellectuals and cultural producers in challenging hegemonic narratives.
Feminist and Postcolonial Perspectives
Simone de Beauvoir

The Second Sex: De Beauvoir's feminist analysis critiques patriarchy and the social construction of gender roles. She advocates for gender equality and the recognition of women's agency in political and social spheres.
Frantz Fanon

The Wretched of the Earth: Fanon's postcolonial theory examines the psychological and social effects of colonialism on oppressed peoples. He calls for decolonization and the reclaiming of cultural identity and political autonomy.
Contemporary Political Thought
John Rawls

Theory of Justice: Rawls' "A Theory of Justice" introduces the concept of justice as fairness, proposing a hypothetical social contract (original position) where individuals agree on principles of justice without knowing their social status.
Amartya Sen

Development as Freedom: Sen's capability approach argues that development should be measured by individuals' capabilities to live freely and pursue valuable life goals. He critiques purely economic metrics and advocates for social justice and human capabilities.
Applications in Modern Politics
Democratic Governance

Electoral Systems: Theories on democracy influence electoral system designs, proportional representation vs. majority systems, and debates on voter participation and representation.
Policy Formulation: Theories of justice and equality inform public policies on welfare, education, healthcare, and environmental protection, balancing individual rights with societal needs.
International Relations

Global Justice: Theories of international relations shape policies on human rights, humanitarian intervention, peacekeeping, and global governance institutions like the United Nations.

Cosmopolitanism vs. Nationalism: Debates on global citizenship, migration, and sovereignty reflect competing theories on global solidarity and national identity.

Conclusion

Political theory continues to provide valuable insights into the nature of power, governance, and societal organization in the modern world. By examining the historical roots and contemporary applications of major political theories—from classical philosophy to critical theory and feminism—we gain a deeper understanding of political dynamics and policy-making. These theoretical frameworks inform debates on democracy, justice, human rights, and global cooperation, guiding efforts to address contemporary challenges and envision more inclusive and equitable political systems. As we explore further in this book, understanding political theory helps navigate complex political landscapes and promote informed civic engagement and policy development in diverse societies.

Chapter 8: Major Political Theories and Thinkers

Political theories provide frameworks for understanding governance, power dynamics, and societal organization. This chapter explores influential political theories and the thinkers who shaped them, examining their contributions to our understanding of politics and governance.

Classical Political Theories
Plato (427-347 BCE)

Theory of Justice: In "The Republic," Plato explores the ideal city-state governed by philosopher-kings. He discusses justice, the role of education in shaping virtuous leaders, and the concept of the philosopher-ruler.
Aristotle (384-322 BCE)

Politics: Aristotle's work delves into different forms of government—monarchy, aristocracy, democracy—and their virtues and vices. He advocates for a mixed form of government that balances the interests of different social classes.
Social Contract Theories
Thomas Hobbes (1588-1679)

Leviathan: Hobbes argues that humans in a state of nature are driven by self-interest and conflict. To avoid chaos, individuals form a social contract, surrendering some freedoms to a sovereign authority for mutual protection and security.
John Locke (1632-1704)

Two Treatises of Government: Locke asserts natural rights (life, liberty, property) and the right of rebellion against tyrannical rule. He proposes a social contract based on consent, with government's legitimacy derived from the people.
Jean-Jacques Rousseau (1712-1778)

The Social Contract: Rousseau posits the concept of the general will, representing the common interests of citizens. He advocates for direct democracy where laws reflect the collective decision-making of the people.
Liberalism and Individualism
John Stuart Mill (1806-1873)

On Liberty: Mill argues for individual liberty as essential for personal development and societal progress. He defends freedom of thought, expression, and action, while advocating for limits on state interference to prevent harm to others.
Isaiah Berlin (1909-1997)

Two Concepts of Liberty: Berlin distinguishes between negative liberty (freedom from external constraints) and positive liberty (ability to achieve one's potential). He critiques authoritarianism and defends pluralism and individual choice.
Marxist and Critical Theories
Karl Marx (1818-1883)

Das Kapital: Marx's critique of capitalism focuses on class struggle and the exploitation of labor. He predicts the eventual collapse of capitalism and the establishment of a classless society based on common ownership.
Antonio Gramsci (1891-1937)

Hegemony and Cultural Marxism: Gramsci's concept of hegemony explores how ruling elites maintain dominance through cultural institutions and ideology. He emphasizes the role of intellectuals and cultural producers in challenging hegemonic narratives.
Feminist and Postcolonial Perspectives
Simone de Beauvoir (1908-1986)

The Second Sex: De Beauvoir's feminist analysis critiques patriarchy and the social construction of gender roles. She advocates for gender equality and the recognition of women's agency in political and social spheres.
Frantz Fanon (1925-1961)

The Wretched of the Earth: Fanon's postcolonial theory examines the psychological and social effects of colonialism on oppressed peoples. He calls for decolonization and the reclaiming of cultural identity and political autonomy.
Contemporary Political Thought
John Rawls (1921-2002)

A Theory of Justice: Rawls introduces the concept of justice as fairness, proposing a hypothetical social contract (original position) where individuals agree on principles of justice without knowing their social status.
Amartya Sen (b. 1933)

Development as Freedom: Sen's capability approach argues that development should be measured by individuals' capabilities to live freely and pursue valuable life goals. He critiques purely economic metrics and advocates for social justice and human capabilities.
Applications in Modern Politics
Democratic Governance

Electoral Systems: Theories on democracy influence electoral system designs, proportional representation vs. majority systems, and debates on voter participation and representation.
Policy Formulation: Theories of justice and equality inform public policies on welfare, education, healthcare, and environmental protection, balancing individual rights with societal needs.
International Relations

Global Justice: Theories of international relations shape policies on human rights, humanitarian intervention, peacekeeping, and global governance institutions like the United Nations.

Cosmopolitanism vs. Nationalism: Debates on global citizenship, migration, and sovereignty reflect competing theories on global solidarity and national identity.

Conclusion

The major political theories and thinkers discussed in this chapter have profoundly influenced our understanding of governance, power, and society. From ancient Greek philosophy to contemporary feminist and postcolonial theories, these frameworks provide valuable insights into political dynamics, policy-making, and the quest for justice and equality in diverse societies. By examining these theories and their applications in modern politics, we gain a deeper appreciation for the complexities of governance and the ongoing debates over democracy, rights, and global cooperation. As we explore further in this book, understanding political theories helps navigate contemporary political landscapes and promotes informed civic engagement and policy development in an ever-changing world.

Chapter 9: Application of Political Theories in Contemporary Politics

Political theories provide foundational principles and frameworks that shape contemporary political discourse, policy-making, and governance practices. This chapter explores how major political theories—from classical to modern perspectives—are applied in analyzing and influencing current political dynamics worldwide.

Classical and Social Contract Theories
Plato and Aristotle's Ideas in Modern Governance

Meritocracy and Leadership: Plato's concept of philosopher-kings and Aristotle's ideas on virtuous governance continue to influence debates on leadership, meritocracy, and political education in democratic and authoritarian regimes alike.
Social Contract and Liberal Democracies

Rights and Liberties: John Locke's emphasis on natural rights and consent of the governed underpins the legal and constitutional frameworks of liberal democracies, shaping laws on individual rights, privacy, and due process.
Liberalism and Individualism
John Stuart Mill's On Liberty

Freedom of Speech and Expression: Mill's defense of freedom of speech informs legal protections and debates on censorship, media regulation, and the boundaries of expression in democratic societies.
Isaiah Berlin's Two Concepts of Liberty

Pluralism and Tolerance: Berlin's distinction between negative and positive liberty guides policies on diversity, multiculturalism, and the protection of minority rights in pluralistic societies.

Marxist and Critical Theories

Karl Marx's Critique of Capitalism

Class Struggle and Economic Policy: Marx's analysis of capitalism informs critiques of income inequality, labor rights movements, and debates over wealth distribution and economic policies in capitalist economies.

Antonio Gramsci's Cultural Hegemony

Media and Cultural Influence: Gramsci's concept of hegemony shapes discussions on media ownership, cultural production, and the influence of dominant ideologies in shaping public opinion and political discourse.

Feminist and Postcolonial Perspectives

Simone de Beauvoir and Gender Equality

Women's Rights and Policy Advocacy: De Beauvoir's feminist critique informs policies on gender equality, reproductive rights, and efforts to combat discrimination and promote women's representation in politics and leadership roles.

Frantz Fanon's Decolonization and Identity Politics

Global Justice and Postcolonialism: Fanon's writings inspire movements for decolonization, indigenous rights, and efforts to address historical injustices and cultural identity in postcolonial societies and international relations.

Contemporary Political Thought

John Rawls' Theory of Justice

Fairness and Social Policies: Rawls' principles of justice as fairness influence debates on social welfare, healthcare reform, affirmative action, and policies aimed at reducing inequality and promoting social justice.
Amartya Sen's Capability Approach

Development and Human Rights: Sen's capability approach informs international development policies, humanitarian interventions, and strategies to enhance human capabilities through education, healthcare, and economic opportunities.
Applications in Global Politics
Democratic Governance and International Relations

Human Rights and Global Governance: Theories of democracy and human rights shape international agreements, peacekeeping missions, and efforts to promote democratic governance and accountability worldwide.
Challenges to Cosmopolitanism and Nationalism

Migration and Sovereignty: Debates over cosmopolitanism versus nationalism influence immigration policies, border controls, and international cooperation on global challenges such as climate change, pandemics, and security threats.
Conclusion
The application of political theories in contemporary politics highlights their relevance in shaping policies, governance structures, and societal values in a rapidly changing world. By examining how these theories inform political ideologies, public policies, and global strategies, we gain insights into the complexities of modern governance and the ongoing quest for justice, equality, and human rights. As we explore further in this book, understanding the application of political theories helps navigate diverse political landscapes, promotes informed decision-making, and fosters dialogue on pressing issues affecting societies worldwide.

Chapter 10: The Structure of Government

The structure of government plays a crucial role in shaping political systems, governance practices, and the distribution of power within societies. This chapter explores different types of government systems, the functions of various branches of government, and their impact on political stability and policy-making.

Types of Government Systems
Democracy

Representative Democracy: Citizens elect representatives to make decisions on their behalf, balancing popular participation with efficient governance.
Direct Democracy: Citizens directly participate in decision-making through referendums or town hall meetings, promoting direct civic engagement but challenging in large populations.
Autocracy

Absolute Monarchy: Power is concentrated in a hereditary monarch, often with limited checks on authority.
Dictatorship: A single leader or party exercises unchecked authority, often suppressing political opposition and civil liberties.
Oligarchy

Rule by Few: Power is held by a small group, often based on wealth, military influence, or familial ties, limiting democratic representation and accountability.
Theocracy

Religious Authority: Governance is guided by religious principles or clerical leadership, intertwining religious and political authority.
Federalism

Division of Powers: Governments are divided between national and regional (state, provincial) levels, allocating specific powers to each while maintaining a unified political system.
Functions and Roles of Government Branches
Executive Branch

Head of State: The president, monarch, or prime minister represents the country domestically and internationally, executing laws and policies.
Executive Agencies: Departments and agencies implement laws and administer government programs, overseeing sectors like defense, health, and transportation.
Legislative Branch

Lawmaking: Parliaments, congresses, or assemblies draft, debate, and pass laws, reflecting public interests and societal needs.
Checks and Balances: Legislators oversee executive actions, confirm judicial appointments, and hold government accountable through hearings and investigations.
Judicial Branch

Interpreting Laws: Courts interpret laws, settle disputes, and ensure constitutional principles are upheld, safeguarding individual rights and liberties.
Judicial Independence: Judges remain impartial and free from political influence, ensuring fair and equitable justice for all citizens.
Political Stability and Governance Efficiency

Constitutional Frameworks

Rule of Law: Constitutions establish legal frameworks, defining government powers, protecting individual rights, and outlining procedures for governance and amendment.
Constitutional Amendments: Flexibility in constitutional amendments allows governments to adapt to societal changes while preserving fundamental principles.
Public Policy and Decision-Making

Policy Formulation: Governments develop policies on economic development, healthcare, education, and social welfare, addressing public needs and promoting societal well-being.
Policy Implementation: Efficient implementation ensures policies are effectively carried out, benefiting citizens and enhancing government credibility.
Challenges and Reform Efforts
Corruption and Accountability

Transparency: Ensuring government transparency and accountability through oversight mechanisms, audits, and whistleblower protections.
Anti-Corruption Measures: Implementing laws and regulations to combat bribery, nepotism, and misuse of public resources, promoting ethical governance practices.
Globalization and Interdependence

International Relations: Governments engage in diplomacy, trade agreements, and international organizations to address global challenges such as climate change, terrorism, and pandemics.
Sovereignty vs. Cooperation: Balancing national sovereignty with international cooperation on issues requiring collective action and shared responsibility.
Conclusion

The structure of government shapes political systems and governance practices, influencing how power is distributed, laws are made, and public policies are implemented. Understanding the types of government systems, roles of government branches, and their impact on political stability and policy-making is essential for navigating complex political landscapes and promoting effective governance. As we explore further in this book, examining the structures of government provides insights into the challenges governments face, the reforms needed for democratic governance, and the evolving role of governance in addressing global issues and societal needs.

Chapter 11: Types of Government Systems

Government systems are fundamental frameworks that determine how political authority is structured, exercised, and distributed within societies. This chapter explores various types of government systems, their characteristics, and the implications for governance, political participation, and societal stability.

Democracy
Representative Democracy

Definition: Citizens elect representatives to make decisions on their behalf through periodic elections.
Features: Emphasis on political participation, protection of individual rights, rule of law, and checks and balances between branches of government.
Examples: United States, United Kingdom, Germany.
Direct Democracy

Definition: Citizens participate directly in decision-making processes, such as referendums or town hall meetings.
Features: High level of citizen engagement, immediate responsiveness to public opinion, but challenging to implement in large populations.
Examples: Switzerland (referendums), ancient Athens (direct assemblies).
Autocracy
Absolute Monarchy

Definition: Power is vested in a hereditary monarch who exercises unchecked authority.

Features: Centralized decision-making, limited political freedoms, authority often based on divine right or tradition.
Examples: Saudi Arabia, Brunei.
Dictatorship

Definition: One leader or a small group holds absolute power, often through coercion, military force, or manipulation of elections.
Features: Suppression of political opposition, limited civil liberties, centralized control over media and institutions.
Examples: North Korea, Zimbabwe under Robert Mugabe.
Oligarchy
Aristocracy

Definition: Political power is concentrated among a privileged class of nobility or wealthy elites.
Features: Limited democratic representation, influence based on wealth, social status, or familial connections.
Examples: Historical ancient Greece (oligarchic city-states).
Plutocracy

Definition: Governance by the wealthy elite who control economic resources and influence political decisions.
Features: Policies favoring economic elites, limited social mobility, potential for corruption and inequality.
Examples: Gilded Age United States, contemporary debates on wealth influence in politics.
Theocracy
Religious Governance
Definition: Political authority is derived from religious institutions or clerical leaders who enforce religious laws.
Features: Integration of religious principles into legal and political systems, potential for religious intolerance.
Examples: Iran (Islamic Republic), Vatican City (Catholic Church).
Federalism

Federal System

Definition: Powers are divided between central (national) and regional (state, provincial) governments, each having specific areas of authority.

Features: Balance between national unity and regional autonomy, constitutional frameworks to define powers and responsibilities.

Examples: United States, Germany, Canada.

Conclusion

The types of government systems outlined in this chapter reflect diverse approaches to governance, each with distinct characteristics, strengths, and challenges. Understanding these systems provides insights into political dynamics, governance practices, and the distribution of power within societies. As we explore further in this book, analyzing different government types helps assess their effectiveness in promoting political stability, protecting individual rights, and addressing societal needs. By examining the evolution and impact of these systems, we gain a deeper appreciation for the complexities of governance and the ongoing quest for effective and responsive political systems in a globalized world.

Chapter 12: Functions and Roles of Various Branches of Government

The branches of government—executive, legislative, and judicial—are essential pillars of governance that balance power, uphold laws, and ensure accountability within political systems. This chapter explores the distinct functions, roles, and interactions of each branch, highlighting their contributions to effective governance and democratic principles.

Executive Branch
Head of State

Role: Represents the country domestically and internationally, embodying national unity and diplomacy.
Responsibilities: Executes laws, commands the military, and conducts foreign relations on behalf of the nation.
Examples: Presidents, monarchs, prime ministers.
Executive Agencies

Role: Implement policies and administer government programs in specific sectors (e.g., defense, healthcare).
Responsibilities: Translate legislative mandates into actions, oversee regulatory compliance, and manage public services.
Examples: Departments of Defense, Health and Human Services.
Legislative Branch
Lawmaking

Role: Drafts, debates, and passes legislation reflecting public interests and societal needs.
Responsibilities: Exercises oversight over the executive branch, approves budgets, and ratifies treaties.
Examples: Parliaments, congresses, assemblies.
Committee System

Role: Specializes in policy areas, conducts hearings, and shapes legislative proposals before they reach the full chamber.
Responsibilities: Investigates issues, deliberates on bills, and provides expertise on diverse policy matters.
Examples: Senate Committees, House Committees.
Judicial Branch
Interpreting Laws

Role: Ensures laws are applied fairly and consistently, resolves disputes, and protects individual rights.
Responsibilities: Reviews the constitutionality of laws, interprets legal texts, and administers justice impartially.
Examples: Supreme Courts, appellate courts, district courts.
Judicial Independence

Role: Operates free from political influence or pressures, ensuring decisions are based on law and justice.
Responsibilities: Upholds the rule of law, safeguards constitutional rights, and checks potential abuses of power.
Examples: Judicial appointments, tenure protections.
Checks and Balances
Executive Oversight

Role: Holds executive branch accountable through hearings, investigations, and budget approvals.
Responsibilities: Checks abuses of power, ensures transparency, and scrutinizes policy implementation.
Examples: Congressional oversight, parliamentary inquiries.

Judicial Review

Role: Reviews laws and executive actions for constitutionality, ensuring adherence to legal principles.
Responsibilities: Protects individual rights, resolves conflicts between branches, and maintains the rule of law.
Examples: Marbury v. Madison (1803), landmark cases on constitutional interpretation.
Constitutional Frameworks
Separation of Powers

Role: Divides governmental authority among branches to prevent concentration of power.
Responsibilities: Maintains institutional independence, fosters cooperation, and balances competing interests.
Examples: Constitutional provisions, checks on executive authority.
Rule of Law

Role: Ensures equality before the law, legal predictability, and accountability of public officials.
Responsibilities: Upholds constitutional principles, protects civil liberties, and promotes justice and fairness.
Examples: Due process, equal protection under the law.
Conclusion
The functions and roles of government branches outlined in this chapter illustrate their critical contributions to governance, democracy, and the rule of law. By examining how each branch operates independently yet collaboratively, we gain insights into the dynamics of political systems and the mechanisms that ensure effective decision-making, accountability, and protection of individual rights. As we explore further in this book, understanding these roles helps navigate complex political landscapes, promote civic engagement, and advocate for responsive and transparent governance practices in diverse societies.

Chapter 13: The Dynamics of Society and Culture

Society and culture are dynamic forces that shape political behavior, influence policy outcomes, and define collective identities. This chapter explores the interplay between societal structures, cultural norms, and political processes, highlighting their impact on governance, social movements, and public policy.

Societal Structures and Political Behavior
Social Institutions

Role: Shape individual beliefs, values, and behaviors that influence political participation and civic engagement.
Examples: Family, education system, religious organizations.
Social Stratification

Role: Division of society into hierarchical layers based on socioeconomic status, influencing access to resources and political influence.
Examples: Class, race, gender.
Cultural Influences on Political Norms
Political Socialization

Role: Process by which individuals acquire political attitudes, values, and behaviors through social interactions and institutional influences.
Examples: Media, peer groups, educational curriculum.
Cultural Dimensions of Politics

Role: Cultural values and beliefs shape political ideologies, policy preferences, and collective identities.
Examples: Individualism vs. collectivism, attitudes towards authority and hierarchy.
Social Movements and Activism
Historical Context

Role: Historical social movements shape current activism, influencing policy agendas and societal norms.
Examples: Civil rights movement, women's suffrage.
Contemporary Activism

Role: Grassroots movements and advocacy efforts mobilize public opinion, challenge power structures, and promote social change.
Examples: Environmental activism, LGBTQ+ rights movements.
Intersectionality and Political Engagement
Identity Politics

Role: Recognition of multiple identities (e.g., race, gender, sexuality) in shaping political identities and policy demands.
Examples: Intersectional feminism, multiculturalism in policy-making.
Representation and Diversity

Role: Importance of diverse representation in political institutions to reflect and address societal diversity and equity concerns.
Examples: Affirmative action, quota systems.
Globalization and Cultural Exchange
Cultural Globalization

Role: Spread of ideas, values, and cultural practices across borders, influencing political ideologies and policy convergence.

Examples: Global media, international human rights norms.
Challenges to Cultural Identity

Role: Resistance to globalization, preservation of cultural heritage, and assertion of local identities in political discourse.
Examples: Indigenous rights movements, cultural protectionism.
Conclusion
The dynamics of society and culture profoundly impact political processes, governance structures, and policy outcomes. By examining how societal structures, cultural norms, and social movements interact with political systems, we gain insights into the complexities of political behavior, identity formation, and policy development. As we explore further in this book, understanding these dynamics helps navigate challenges of social change, promote inclusive governance, and foster dialogue on the evolving role of culture in shaping political landscapes and collective aspirations in diverse societies.

Chapter 14: Sociology and Its Impact on Politics

Sociology provides critical insights into how societal structures, group dynamics, and collective behavior shape political processes, policy outcomes, and governance. This chapter explores the intersection of sociology with politics, highlighting its influence on understanding social movements, political behavior, and policy formulation.

Societal Structures and Political Behavior
Social Institutions

Role: Influence political attitudes and behaviors through socialization processes within institutions such as family, education, and religion.
Examples: Impact of family values on voting patterns, educational attainment influencing political engagement.
Social Stratification

Role: Division of society into hierarchical groups based on socioeconomic status, race, gender, and other factors that influence access to political power and resources.
Examples: Class-based political mobilization, racial disparities in political representation.
Group Dynamics and Political Mobilization
Social Movements

Role: Collective actions driven by shared grievances, identities, or ideologies that challenge existing power structures and advocate for social change.
Examples: Civil rights movements, environmental activism, labor movements.
Political Participation

Role: Study of factors influencing voter turnout, political engagement, and civic participation within diverse social groups.
Examples: Youth voter mobilization, impact of social media on political activism.
Identity Politics and Social Justice Movements
Intersectionality

Role: Recognition of overlapping identities (e.g., race, gender, sexuality) and their impact on political identities, policy priorities, and social movements.
Examples: Intersectional feminism, LGBTQ+ rights advocacy in political platforms.
Social Justice

Role: Sociology's contribution to understanding inequalities, discrimination, and policies aimed at promoting equity and justice in society.
Examples: Policies addressing income inequality, affirmative action in higher education.
Globalization and Social Change
Cultural Globalization

Role: Spread of cultural norms, values, and social movements across borders, influencing political ideologies and global governance.
Examples: Global human rights movements, impact of global media on political perceptions.
Transnational Advocacy Networks

Role: Collaboration across borders among NGOs, activists, and international organizations to influence global policies and address transnational issues.
Examples: Climate change activism, global health initiatives.
Sociology in Policy Formulation
Evidence-Based Policy

Role: Use of sociological research and data to inform policy decisions, address social problems, and promote effective governance.
Examples: Poverty reduction strategies, criminal justice reform based on social science research.
Public Opinion and Policy Support

Role: Sociology's role in understanding public attitudes, perceptions, and support for policies, shaping government responsiveness and accountability.
Examples: Public opinion polls, focus groups in policy-making processes.
Conclusion
Sociology provides invaluable perspectives on how social structures, group dynamics, and cultural factors influence political processes and policy outcomes. By exploring the intersection of sociology with politics, we deepen our understanding of social movements, political behavior, and governance challenges in diverse societies. As we continue to delve into this book, examining sociology's impact on politics helps navigate complexities of social change, promote inclusive policies, and foster dialogue on the evolving role of sociology in shaping political landscapes and advancing societal well-being.

Chapter 15: How Societal Structures Influence Political Behavior

Societal structures play a pivotal role in shaping political behavior by influencing attitudes, values, and actions of individuals within a society. This chapter examines how various societal factors impact political behavior, participation, and outcomes.

Family Dynamics and Political Socialization
Role of Family

Influence: Transmission of political values, attitudes, and party affiliations from parents to children.
Examples: Household discussions on politics, parental voting behavior influencing children's political views.
Generational Effects

Impact: Long-term influence of family backgrounds on political preferences and voter turnout across different generations.
Examples: Changes in political allegiance over time, generational shifts in voting patterns.
Education and Civic Engagement

Educational Attainment

Effect: Higher levels of education correlate with increased political knowledge, participation, and engagement.
Examples: Impact of educational curriculum on civic awareness, college-educated voters' participation rates.
Political Literacy

Role: Acquisition of knowledge about political processes, institutions, and policies through formal education.
Examples: Civics education programs, political science courses in universities.
Religious Institutions and Political Ideologies
Religious Affiliation

Influence: Alignment of religious beliefs with political ideologies and policy preferences.
Examples: Religious voter blocs, influence of religious leaders on political discourse.
Moral and Ethical Values

Impact: Integration of religious teachings into moral frameworks that guide political decision-making and policy stances.
Examples: Views on social issues (e.g., abortion, same-sex marriage) influenced by religious teachings.
Economic Status and Political Participation
Income and Wealth

Effect: Disparities in political influence based on economic resources, access to political networks, and campaign contributions.
Examples: Influence of wealthy donors on political campaigns, advocacy by business groups.
Social Class

Role: Differences in political attitudes and behaviors among social classes based on economic status and occupational roles.
Examples: Class-based voting patterns, policies addressing income inequality.
Cultural Diversity and Political Identity
Ethnicity and Race

Influence: Political identities shaped by racial and ethnic backgrounds, affecting voting behavior and policy priorities.
Examples: Minority voter turnout, political representation of marginalized communities.
Gender and Political Participation

Impact: Differences in political engagement, representation, and policy interests between genders.
Examples: Gender gaps in voter turnout, advocacy for women's rights and gender equality.
Technology and Changing Political Landscape
Digital Media

Effect: Influence of social media, online platforms, and digital communications on political mobilization and information sharing.
Examples: Impact of viral campaigns, digital activism in political movements.
Globalization

Role: Integration of global issues and perspectives into local political discourse, shaping policy responses and international cooperation.
Examples: Transnational advocacy networks, global solidarity movements.
Conclusion

Societal structures exert profound influences on political behavior, shaping individuals' attitudes, identities, and actions within political systems. By examining how family dynamics, educational experiences, religious affiliations, economic factors, cultural diversity, and technological advancements impact political engagement, we gain insights into the complexities of democratic participation and governance. As we delve deeper into this book, exploring the dynamics between societal structures and political behavior helps navigate challenges, promote inclusive civic participation, and foster informed decision-making in evolving societies.

Chapter 16: Role of Social Institutions (Family, Education, Religion)

Social institutions—such as family, education, and religion—play crucial roles in shaping societal values, beliefs, and behaviors, including their impact on political attitudes, civic engagement, and governance. This chapter explores how these institutions influence political dynamics and shape individual and collective identities.

Family and Political Socialization
Transmission of Values

Role: Families impart political beliefs, attitudes, and values to children through upbringing and socialization.
Examples: Discussions about civic responsibility, exposure to political events and discussions at home.
Generational Influence

Effect: Continuation of familial political traditions and voting behaviors across generations.
Examples: Voting patterns influenced by family background, generational shifts in political allegiances.
Education and Civic Engagement
Knowledge Acquisition

Role: Formal education provides knowledge about political systems, processes, and citizenship responsibilities.
Examples: Civics education, political science courses, debates and discussions in schools.
Civic Participation

Impact: Higher levels of education correlate with increased political awareness, voter turnout, and engagement in public affairs.
Examples: Influence of educational attainment on political activism, advocacy for policy change.
Religion and Political Ideologies
Religious Affiliation

Influence: Alignment of religious beliefs with political values, influencing policy preferences and electoral choices.
Examples: Moral considerations in voting, religious leaders' influence on political discourse.
Moral Frameworks

Effect: Religious teachings shape ethical perspectives and moral positions on social and political issues.
Examples: Views on abortion, LGBTQ+ rights, and social justice policies influenced by religious doctrines.
Institutional Roles in Social Cohesion
Social Cohesion

Role: Institutions foster social bonds and collective identities, promoting unity and cooperation within communities.
Examples: Community service projects, charitable initiatives supported by religious organizations.
Integration and Diversity

Impact: Institutions contribute to social integration and cultural diversity, shaping inclusive citizenship and civic participation.
Examples: Multicultural education programs, religious tolerance and interfaith dialogue initiatives.
Challenges and Evolving Roles
Adaptation to Change

Role: Institutions adapt to societal changes and technological advancements, influencing political engagement and governance.
Examples: Use of digital platforms in education, social media's impact on religious outreach and activism.
Accountability and Trust

Effect: Institutions' transparency, accountability, and public trust influence their effectiveness in shaping political attitudes and behaviors.
Examples: Public perceptions of institutional integrity, reforms to enhance accountability in education and religious organizations.
Conclusion
Social institutions—family, education, and religion—serve as foundational pillars that shape societal norms, values, and political behaviors. By examining their roles in political socialization, civic engagement, and community cohesion, we gain insights into the complex interactions between individuals, communities, and political systems. As we continue to explore this book, understanding the influence of social institutions helps navigate challenges in governance, promote civic responsibility, and foster inclusive societies where diverse perspectives contribute to democratic processes and collective well-being.

Chapter 17: Anthropological Insights into Political Systems

Anthropology offers unique perspectives on how cultural norms, social structures, and human behaviors influence the organization and functioning of political systems. This chapter explores anthropological insights into various aspects of political systems, highlighting cultural diversity, power dynamics, and the evolution of governance.

Cultural Dimensions of Politics
Cultural Relativism

Perspective: Anthropology emphasizes understanding political systems within their cultural contexts, respecting diverse norms and values.
Examples: Study of indigenous governance structures, cultural practices influencing political decision-making.
Political Rituals and Symbolism

Observations: Anthropologists analyze rituals, ceremonies, and symbolic gestures that reinforce political authority and social cohesion.
Examples: Coronation ceremonies, state-sponsored festivals, public demonstrations of power.
Power and Authority
Legitimacy and Governance

Analysis: Anthropological studies examine sources of political legitimacy, including tradition, charisma, and institutional authority.
Examples: Tribal leadership systems, charismatic leaders in modern politics.

Hierarchy and Social Organization

Observations: Anthropologists explore hierarchical structures within societies, reflecting power relations and distribution of authority.
Examples: Caste systems, class divisions influencing political participation.
Kinship and Political Alliances
Kinship Networks

Impact: Anthropological research highlights how kinship ties influence political alliances, coalition-building, and succession.
Examples: Nepotism in political appointments, family-based political dynasties.
Marriage and Political Strategies

Insights: Analysis of marriage alliances as political strategies to strengthen familial ties and consolidate power.
Examples: Diplomatic marriages, alliances between ruling families.
Conflict and Resolution
Ethnicity and Identity Politics

Studies: Anthropological perspectives on ethnic identities, conflicts, and political mobilization based on cultural affiliations.
Examples: Ethnic minority rights movements, identity-based political parties.
Mediation and Dispute Resolution

Observations: Examination of traditional and modern methods of conflict resolution, addressing disputes within political contexts.
Examples: Tribal councils, international mediation in ethnic conflicts.

Evolution of Political Institutions
Historical Perspectives

Anthropological Approaches: Longitudinal studies trace the evolution of political institutions, examining adaptive strategies and continuity.
Examples: Evolution of democratic practices, resilience of traditional governance in modern contexts.
Globalization and Indigenous Governance

Impact: Anthropological insights on globalization's influence on indigenous governance structures and cultural resilience.
Examples: Indigenous rights movements, international recognition of indigenous political autonomy.
Conclusion
Anthropological insights enrich our understanding of political systems by highlighting cultural diversity, power dynamics, and adaptive strategies across societies. By exploring how anthropology examines political rituals, power relations, kinship networks, and conflict resolution mechanisms, we gain deeper insights into the complexities of governance and societal organization. As we delve further into this book, anthropological perspectives contribute to navigating challenges in global politics, fostering cultural understanding, and promoting inclusive governance that respects and incorporates diverse cultural values and practices.

Chapter 18: Cultural Influences on Political Norms and Values

Cultural influences significantly shape political norms, values, and behaviors within societies. This chapter explores how cultural dynamics impact political ideologies, governance practices, and policy-making processes, highlighting the interplay between cultural heritage, societal norms, and political developments.

Cultural Diversity in Political Ideologies
Cultural Worldviews

Impact: Cultural beliefs and values shape political ideologies, influencing perspectives on governance, rights, and societal goals.
Examples: Individualism vs. collectivism, attitudes towards authority and hierarchy.
Ethnicity and National Identity

Role: Ethnic diversity contributes to varied political identities, affecting policy preferences and electoral outcomes.
Examples: Nationalist movements, multiculturalism in policy-making.
Traditional Practices and Political Institutions
Customary Law and Governance

Observations: Cultural norms and customary practices influence legal systems and governance structures, shaping local political processes.

Examples: Tribal councils, customary dispute resolution mechanisms.
Religious Values in Politics

Analysis: Influence of religious teachings and moral frameworks on political norms, policies, and societal attitudes.
Examples: Religious conservatism, secularism debates.
Cultural Heritage and Civic Engagement
Historical Narratives

Impact: Shared historical experiences shape collective memory and political solidarity, influencing civic engagement.
Examples: National independence movements, commemorative ceremonies.
Art, Media, and Political Discourse

Role: Cultural expressions through art, literature, and media influence public opinion, political debates, and social movements.
Examples: Political satire, cultural representations in media.
Gender Roles and Political Participation
Cultural Norms

Observations: Cultural expectations regarding gender roles influence women's participation in politics and leadership roles.
Examples: Gender quotas, cultural barriers to women's political empowerment.
Feminist Movements

Impact: Feminist movements challenge cultural norms, advocating for gender equality in political representation and policy-making.
Examples: Women's rights activism, gender mainstreaming in governance.
Globalization and Cultural Adaptation

Cultural Hybridity

Effect: Globalization facilitates cultural exchange and adaptation, influencing political norms and values.
Examples: Global human rights standards, Western influence on democratic ideals.
Resistance and Cultural Revival

Role: Cultural movements resist globalization's homogenizing effects, advocating for cultural preservation and political autonomy.
Examples: Indigenous rights movements, cultural revitalization initiatives.
Conclusion
Cultural influences on political norms and values shape the fabric of societies, influencing governance structures, policy priorities, and civic engagement. By examining how cultural diversity, traditional practices, religious beliefs, and global influences impact political ideologies and behaviors, we gain insights into the complexities of political dynamics. As we continue to explore this book, understanding cultural influences on political norms fosters dialogue on inclusive governance, cultural rights, and the promotion of democratic values that respect and reflect diverse cultural identities in global contexts.

Chapter 19: Social Movements and Activism

Social movements and activism play pivotal roles in shaping political agendas, challenging power structures, and advocating for social change. This chapter explores the dynamics of social movements, their historical contexts, strategies, and impacts on policy-making and societal transformation.

Historical Context of Social Movements
Emergence and Evolution

Overview: Historical roots of social movements, from civil rights struggles to labor movements, shaping contemporary activism.
Examples: Suffrage movement, anti-apartheid struggle, environmental movements.
Global Perspectives

Impact: Transnational movements and solidarity efforts across borders, addressing global issues and promoting international cooperation.
Examples: Global climate strikes, human rights campaigns.
Types and Strategies of Social Movements
Issue-Based Movements

Focus: Movements addressing specific social, economic, or political issues, mobilizing public support and advocating for policy change.
Examples: LGBTQ+ rights movements, healthcare reform campaigns.
Identity-Based Movements

Emphasis: Movements based on collective identities (e.g., race, gender, ethnicity), challenging discrimination and promoting equality.
Examples: Black Lives Matter, Indigenous rights movements.
Role of Activism in Policy-Making
Policy Advocacy

Strategies: Activists engage in lobbying, protest actions, and legal challenges to influence policy decisions and legislative agendas.
Examples: Marches, sit-ins, grassroots campaigns.
Public Opinion and Media Influence

Impact: Activists use media platforms and public discourse to raise awareness, shape narratives, and mobilize public support.
Examples: Social media campaigns, viral hashtags.
Challenges and Successes
Challenges

Obstacles: Resistance from authorities, funding constraints, internal divisions, and public skepticism.
Examples: Government crackdowns on protests, backlash from opponents.
Success Stories

Achievements: Examples of social movements achieving policy reforms, societal shifts, and cultural change through sustained activism.

Examples: Marriage equality, environmental protection laws.
Intersectionality and Coalition-Building
Intersectional Movements

Approach: Movements addressing multiple forms of oppression and identities, fostering solidarity and inclusive advocacy.
Examples: Women's rights movements, intersectional feminism.
Coalition Strategies

Collaboration: Building alliances across diverse groups and movements to amplify voices and broaden support for shared goals.
Examples: Labor unions collaborating with environmental activists, civil rights groups forming alliances.
Future Directions and Impact
Innovations in Activism

Trends: Utilization of digital tools, online organizing, and new tactics to mobilize and sustain momentum in movements.
Examples: Online petitions, crowdfunding platforms.
Global Movements

Influence: Role of global movements in addressing transnational issues, advocating for human rights, and challenging global power dynamics.
Examples: Youth climate movements, global anti-corruption campaigns.
Conclusion

Social movements and activism are essential forces driving social change, challenging injustices, and advancing democratic values. By examining their historical evolution, strategic approaches, and impacts on policy-making, we gain insights into their transformative potential and ongoing relevance in addressing contemporary challenges. As we explore further in this book, understanding social movements and activism inspires engagement, promotes civic participation, and underscores the importance of collective action in shaping equitable and inclusive societies.

Chapter 20: Historical and Contemporary Social Movements

Social movements have shaped societies throughout history, challenging norms, advocating for rights, and driving significant social change. This chapter examines key historical movements and their contemporary counterparts, highlighting their impact, strategies, and enduring legacies.

Civil Rights Movement
Historical Context

Overview: Emergence in the mid-20th century United States, advocating for racial equality, desegregation, and civil liberties.
Examples: Montgomery Bus Boycott, March on Washington, Voting Rights Act of 1965.
Legacy and Impact

Achievements: Legal and societal transformations, including landmark civil rights legislation and societal shifts in racial attitudes.
Examples: Integration of schools, voting rights protections, cultural empowerment.
Women's Suffrage Movement
Historical Context

Overview: Campaigns for women's right to vote and broader gender equality, spanning the late 19th to early 20th centuries.
Examples: Seneca Falls Convention, Suffrage Parade, 19th Amendment (1920).
Impact and Legacy

Achievements: Expansion of political rights for women, paving the way for subsequent feminist movements and policy reforms.
Examples: Equal Pay Act, reproductive rights advocacy, women in leadership roles.
Labor Movements
Historical Context

Overview: Worker rights movements advocating for better working conditions, fair wages, and labor rights protections.
Examples: Industrial Revolution labor protests, trade unions, International Workers' Day.
Contemporary Issues

Challenges: Globalization's impact on labor rights, gig economy challenges, and evolving strategies in union organizing.
Examples: Fight for $15 movement, worker strikes for better benefits, global solidarity campaigns.
Environmental Movements
Historical Roots

Overview: Conservation and environmental protection movements advocating for sustainable practices and ecological preservation.
Examples: Sierra Club, Earth Day, Clean Air Act (1970).
Modern Challenges

Emerging Issues: Climate change activism, biodiversity conservation, and global efforts for environmental justice.
Examples: Youth climate strikes, international agreements like the Paris Agreement, renewable energy advocacy.
LGBTQ+ Rights Movements
Historical Struggles

Overview: Movements advocating for LGBTQ+ rights, including decriminalization, marriage equality, and anti-discrimination protections.
Examples: Stonewall Riots, AIDS activism, Obergefell v. Hodges (2015).
Progress and Ongoing Advocacy

Achievements: Legal victories, societal acceptance, and ongoing advocacy for transgender rights, LGBTQ+ youth support, and global equality.
Examples: Pride marches, legislative wins for LGBTQ+ rights, activism against conversion therapy.
Conclusion

Historical and contemporary social movements have been instrumental in advancing rights, challenging injustices, and shaping progressive social change globally. By examining their origins, strategies, impacts, and ongoing challenges, we recognize their enduring relevance in promoting equality, justice, and human dignity. As we delve into this chapter, understanding the evolution and diversity of social movements inspires continued engagement, solidarity across diverse causes, and collective action towards building inclusive societies where rights and freedoms are upheld for all.

Chapter 21: The Role of Activism in Shaping Policy and Public Opinion

Activism plays a crucial role in influencing policy decisions and shaping public opinion on various social, political, and environmental issues. This chapter explores how activism mobilizes public support, challenges existing norms, and drives legislative changes through advocacy, protest, and grassroots campaigns.

Influence on Policy-Making
Advocacy Campaigns

Strategies: Activists use lobbying, petitions, and direct engagement with policymakers to advocate for policy reforms.
Examples: Advocacy for healthcare reform, environmental protection laws, and civil rights legislation.
Legal Challenges

Impact: Activists initiate legal actions, lawsuits, and court challenges to address systemic injustices and enforce constitutional rights.
Examples: Landmark Supreme Court cases, litigation against discriminatory practices.
Mobilizing Public Support
Grassroots Movements

Community Organizing: Activists mobilize communities, educate the public, and build coalitions to amplify their voices and influence.

Examples: Community protests, neighborhood campaigns for local issues.
Media and Communication

Public Awareness: Activists use media platforms, social networks, and traditional media to raise awareness and shape public discourse.
Examples: Social media campaigns, viral videos, op-eds in newspapers.
Shifting Public Opinion
Narrative Framing

Storytelling: Activists frame issues through compelling narratives that resonate with public values and emotions, shifting attitudes.
Examples: Humanizing stories of individuals affected by policies, narratives of social justice and equality.
Cultural Influence

Artistic Expression: Activists use art, music, and cultural expressions to challenge norms, inspire solidarity, and foster empathy.
Examples: Protest songs, street art, performance art in activism.
Challenges and Resilience
Opposition and Backlash

Resistance: Activists face opposition from vested interests, political adversaries, and public skepticism, requiring resilience.
Examples: Counter-protests, legal restrictions on protest rights.
Adaptation and Innovation

Strategic Evolution: Activists innovate tactics, leverage technology, and adapt strategies to navigate challenges and sustain momentum.
Examples: Digital organizing tools, decentralized leadership models, creative protest tactics.
Impact on Global Issues
International Solidarity

Global Movements: Activists collaborate across borders to address transnational issues like climate change, human rights abuses, and global inequalities.
Examples: Global climate strikes, international human rights campaigns.
Policy Advocacy

International Advocacy: Activists engage in international forums, lobby governments, and influence global policies and agreements.
Examples: UN conventions, international NGO campaigns.
Conclusion
Activism is a catalyst for social change, shaping policy agendas, influencing public opinion, and fostering civic engagement worldwide. By examining its role in policy-making, public mobilization, and cultural transformation, we understand its power to challenge injustices, promote rights, and advocate for a more equitable and inclusive society. As we explore this chapter, recognizing activism's diverse strategies and global impact inspires collective action, solidarity across movements, and continued efforts towards building a better world based on justice, equality, and human rights.

Chapter 22: Basic Economic Principles and Their Political Implications

Understanding economic principles is essential for comprehending the underpinnings of political decisions, policies, and societal well-being. This chapter delves into fundamental economic concepts and examines how they shape political discourse, policy-making, and societal outcomes.

Supply and Demand
Market Forces

Concept: Interaction of supply and demand determines prices, allocation of resources, and economic efficiency.
Political Implications: Policies influencing market competition, regulation, and consumer protection.
Price Mechanism

Function: Prices convey information and incentives, guiding production, consumption, and investment decisions.
Political Implications: Government intervention, price controls, and fiscal policies impacting market stability.
Macroeconomic Principles
Growth and Output

Objective: Economic growth measures national output, productivity, and standards of living.

Political Implications: Fiscal policies (taxation, spending), monetary policies (interest rates), and infrastructure investments.
Inflation and Unemployment

Challenges: Balancing price stability (inflation control) and full employment.
Political Implications: Central bank policies (monetary policy), labor market regulations, and social safety nets.
Fiscal Policy
Government Spending and Taxation

Role: Fiscal policy influences aggregate demand, economic growth, and income distribution.
Political Implications: Budget priorities, deficit management, and redistributive policies.
Public Debt

Impact: Accumulation of government debt affects fiscal sustainability and future policy options.
Political Implications: Debt management strategies, austerity measures, and intergenerational equity.
Monetary Policy
Interest Rates and Money Supply

Tool: Central banks use monetary policy to manage inflation, support economic growth, and stabilize financial markets.
Political Implications: Independence of central banks, inflation targeting, and financial stability regulations.
Exchange Rates

Importance: Exchange rate policies influence trade balances, international competitiveness, and economic openness.
Political Implications: Currency interventions, trade agreements, and globalization impacts.
Economic Systems and Ideologies

Capitalism vs. Socialism

Ideological Divide: Debate over market efficiency, income distribution, and government intervention.
Political Implications: Policy debates on privatization, welfare programs, and income redistribution.
Globalization

Integration: Economic globalization connects markets, economies, and societies globally.
Political Implications: Trade agreements, international economic cooperation, and challenges to national sovereignty.
Conclusion
Basic economic principles are foundational to understanding the dynamics of politics, policy-making, and societal outcomes. By exploring how concepts like supply and demand, fiscal and monetary policies, and economic ideologies influence political decisions and societal well-being, we gain insights into the complexities of governance and economic management. As we delve further into this chapter, understanding these principles equips us to analyze policy debates, assess economic policies' impacts, and advocate for strategies that promote sustainable economic development and inclusive prosperity.

Chapter 23: How Economic Policies Affect Societal Wellbeing

Economic policies wield significant influence over the quality of life, prosperity, and social outcomes within societies. This chapter examines the multifaceted impacts of economic policies on various aspects of societal wellbeing, from income distribution to public health and beyond.

Income Distribution and Poverty
Income Disparities

Impact: Economic policies shape income distribution, affecting wealth accumulation and social mobility.
Examples: Taxation policies, minimum wage laws, social safety nets.
Poverty Alleviation

Strategies: Economic policies target poverty reduction through targeted assistance programs and economic empowerment initiatives.
Examples: Universal basic income, job creation programs, access to education and healthcare.
Employment and Labor Market Dynamics
Job Creation

Policy Interventions: Economic policies stimulate employment growth through fiscal incentives, infrastructure investments, and labor market reforms.

Examples: Employment subsidies, vocational training programs, labor market regulations.
Quality of Work

Impact: Policies influence working conditions, job security, and wages, shaping overall job satisfaction and economic security.
Examples: Workplace safety regulations, fair labor standards, collective bargaining rights.
Public Health and Social Services
Healthcare Access

Policy Implications: Economic policies affect access to healthcare services, affordability, and healthcare system sustainability.
Examples: Healthcare financing reforms, insurance coverage expansions, public health investments.
Education and Human Capital Development

Investment Strategies: Economic policies promote access to quality education, skills development, and lifelong learning opportunities.
Examples: Education funding, student loan programs, vocational training subsidies.
Housing and Infrastructure
Affordable Housing

Policy Initiatives: Economic policies address housing affordability, urban development, and sustainable housing solutions.
Examples: Housing subsidies, zoning regulations, public-private partnerships.
Infrastructure Development

Impact: Investments in infrastructure enhance economic productivity, mobility, and environmental sustainability.

Examples: Transportation projects, energy infrastructure upgrades, digital connectivity initiatives.
Environmental Sustainability
Green Policies

Environmental Impact: Economic policies promote sustainability through incentives for renewable energy, emissions reductions, and conservation efforts.
Examples: Carbon pricing mechanisms, environmental regulations, green technology investments.
Climate Resilience

Adaptation Strategies: Economic policies address climate change impacts, promoting resilience in infrastructure, agriculture, and natural resource management.
Examples: Climate adaptation funds, disaster risk reduction strategies, sustainable land use policies.
Conclusion
Economic policies are pivotal in shaping societal wellbeing by influencing income distribution, employment opportunities, access to essential services, and environmental sustainability. By examining their impacts across these dimensions, we recognize the critical role of policy-making in fostering inclusive growth, reducing inequalities, and promoting sustainable development. As we explore further in this chapter, understanding how economic policies affect societal wellbeing informs policy debates, guides decision-making, and underscores the importance of equitable and sustainable economic strategies for fostering thriving and resilient communities.

Chapter 24: Public Policy: Crafting the Common Good

Public policy plays a crucial role in shaping societal values, addressing collective needs, and advancing the common good. This chapter explores the principles, processes, and outcomes of public policy-making, focusing on its role in promoting social justice, equity, and sustainable development.

Principles of Public Policy
Social Justice

Objective: Policies aim to ensure fairness, equal opportunities, and rights for all members of society.
Examples: Anti-discrimination laws, affirmative action programs, access to justice initiatives.
Equity

Goal: Policies strive to reduce disparities and promote fairness in resource distribution and access to opportunities.
Examples: Income redistribution policies, education funding equity, healthcare access reforms.
Policy-Making Processes
Policy Formulation

Process: Identification of issues, research, stakeholder consultation, and drafting of policy proposals.
Examples: Government task forces, policy research institutes, public consultations.

Policy Implementation

Execution: Translation of policy into programs, regulations, and actions to achieve intended outcomes.
Examples: Government agencies, regulatory bodies, implementation frameworks.
Policy Evaluation

Assessment: Monitoring and evaluation of policy effectiveness, impact assessment, and feedback mechanisms.
Examples: Performance indicators, outcome evaluations, policy reviews.
Governance and Accountability
Democratic Governance

Principles: Policies reflect democratic principles, transparency, and accountability to citizens.
Examples: Electoral mandates, public hearings, freedom of information laws.
Public Sector Ethics

Standards: Policies uphold ethical standards, integrity, and accountability in public service delivery.
Examples: Code of conduct for public officials, anti-corruption measures, whistleblower protection.
Policy Areas Promoting Common Good
Healthcare

Objectives: Policies ensure access to quality healthcare services, promote public health, and address healthcare disparities.
Examples: Universal healthcare systems, disease prevention programs, mental health services.
Education

Priorities: Policies focus on equitable access to education, quality teaching standards, and lifelong learning opportunities.
Examples: Education reforms, student support programs, literacy campaigns.
Social Welfare

Initiatives: Policies support vulnerable populations, provide social safety nets, and address poverty and homelessness.
Examples: Social security programs, unemployment benefits, housing assistance.
Sustainable Development Goals (SDGs)
Global Commitments

Agenda: Policies align with international commitments to achieve sustainable development, climate action, and global cooperation.
Examples: SDGs implementation, climate change adaptation strategies, biodiversity conservation policies.
Local and Global Impact

Integration: Policies integrate local priorities with global sustainability goals, promoting inclusive and environmentally responsible development.
Examples: Local Agenda 21 initiatives, sustainable cities planning, global climate agreements.
Conclusion

Public policy serves as a cornerstone for advancing the common good, fostering inclusive societies, and addressing complex challenges facing communities worldwide. By examining its principles, processes, and impacts across key policy areas, we recognize its transformative potential in promoting social justice, equity, and sustainable development. As we explore this chapter further, understanding the dynamics of public policy-making informs civic engagement, advocates for policy reforms, and underscores the imperative of collaborative efforts towards building resilient and thriving communities for present and future generations.

Chapter 25: The Policy-Making Process

The policy-making process is a dynamic and multifaceted journey involving various stages, stakeholders, and factors. This chapter provides an in-depth exploration of how policies are formulated, implemented, and evaluated, highlighting key actors, methods, and challenges inherent in the process.

Stages of Policy-Making
Agenda Setting

Initiation: Identification of issues requiring policy attention, influenced by public demand, crises, or political priorities. Examples: Public outcry, expert recommendations, political campaigns.
Policy Formulation

Development: Crafting policy proposals, involving research, consultation with stakeholders, and drafting legislative or administrative frameworks.
Examples: Task forces, policy papers, expert committees.
Decision-Making

Adoption: Selection of preferred policy options through legislative processes, executive orders, or regulatory decisions.
Examples: Parliamentary debates, executive decrees, regulatory rulemaking.
Implementation

Execution: Operationalizing policies through programs, regulations, and administrative actions to achieve intended goals.
Examples: Government agencies, service delivery mechanisms, infrastructure projects.
Evaluation

Assessment: Monitoring and assessing policy effectiveness, impacts on stakeholders, and alignment with objectives.
Examples: Performance metrics, impact evaluations, policy reviews.
Actors in the Policy Process
Government Institutions

Roles: Legislatures, executive agencies, and judiciary contribute to policy formulation, enactment, and oversight.
Examples: Ministries, congressional committees, regulatory bodies.
Interest Groups

Influence: Advocacy organizations, industry associations, and civil society groups shape policy agendas and outcomes through lobbying and mobilization.

Examples: Trade unions, environmental NGOs, professional associations.
Academic and Research Community

Expertise: Researchers, scholars, and think tanks provide evidence-based analysis, policy recommendations, and evaluations.
Examples: Policy research institutes, universities, economic consultants.
Public Opinion and Media

Public Discourse: Public perceptions, media coverage, and social media shape policy debates, influencing decision-makers and agenda setting.
Examples: Opinion polls, media campaigns, social media activism.
Challenges in Policy-Making
Complexity and Uncertainty

Issues: Addressing multifaceted problems with uncertain outcomes requires adaptive policy approaches.
Examples: Climate change, technological disruptions, global health crises.
Political Interests and Power Dynamics

Influence: Competing interests, ideological divides, and power struggles influence policy priorities and decision-making processes.
Examples: Partisan politics, corporate influence, grassroots movements.
Implementation Gaps

Execution: Challenges in translating policy intentions into effective actions due to resource constraints, bureaucratic inefficiencies, and resistance to change.

Examples: Funding shortages, capacity limitations, administrative hurdles.
Policy Innovation and Adaptation
Innovative Approaches

Adaptation: Policy experimentation, pilot projects, and adaptive governance foster innovation and responsiveness to evolving challenges.
Examples: Policy labs, agile governance frameworks, digital transformation strategies.
Learning from Experience

Feedback: Iterative policy cycles, learning from successes and failures, and adapting strategies based on evidence and stakeholder feedback.
Examples: Policy evaluations, lessons learned workshops, policy revisions.
Conclusion
The policy-making process is pivotal in addressing societal challenges, promoting public welfare, and advancing collective goals. By examining its stages, stakeholders, and challenges, we gain insights into its complexities and opportunities for enhancing governance effectiveness, promoting inclusive decision-making, and achieving sustainable development. As we delve into this chapter, understanding the policy-making process informs civic engagement, fosters policy innovation, and underscores the importance of collaborative efforts in shaping responsive and resilient governance frameworks for the benefit of all stakeholders.

Chapter 26: Analysis of Major Public Policies and Their Impacts

This chapter delves into the examination and evaluation of significant public policies, analyzing their formulation, implementation, and outcomes across diverse sectors. By studying these policies, we gain insights into their effectiveness, challenges, and broader implications for society.

Health Care Policy
Policy Overview

Objectives: Ensuring access to affordable healthcare, improving public health outcomes, and addressing healthcare disparities.

Examples: Affordable Care Act (ACA), universal healthcare systems, public health emergency responses.
Impact Assessment

Achievements: Expanded healthcare coverage, reduced uninsured rates, improved health outcomes.
Challenges: Cost containment, healthcare quality disparities, political opposition.
Education Policy
Policy Goals

Priorities: Promoting equitable access to quality education, enhancing educational outcomes, and addressing systemic inequalities.
Examples: Education reform initiatives, funding formulas, early childhood education programs.
Outcome Evaluation

Successes: Increased graduation rates, improved academic achievement, enhanced workforce readiness.
Challenges: Achievement gaps, funding adequacy, teacher shortages.
Environmental Policy
Policy Focus

Objectives: Mitigating climate change, conserving natural resources, promoting sustainable development.
Examples: Paris Agreement commitments, clean energy initiatives, environmental regulations.
Environmental Impact

Progress: Emissions reductions, renewable energy adoption, ecosystem conservation.
Challenges: Regulatory rollbacks, global coordination, climate adaptation.
Economic Policy

Policy Objectives

Goals: Stimulating economic growth, reducing unemployment, and promoting equitable prosperity.
Examples: Fiscal stimulus packages, monetary policy adjustments, trade agreements.
Economic Outcomes

Achievements: GDP growth, job creation, poverty reduction.
Challenges: Income inequality, economic volatility, global economic integration.
Social Welfare Policy
Policy Aims

Priorities: Providing safety nets, reducing poverty, and supporting vulnerable populations.
Examples: Social security programs, unemployment benefits, housing assistance.
Impact Analysis

Success Stories: Poverty alleviation, improved living standards, social cohesion.
Challenges: Program sustainability, eligibility criteria, intergenerational equity.
Technology and Innovation Policy
Policy Objectives

Focus Areas: Promoting research and development, fostering technological innovation, and addressing digital divides.
Examples: R&D tax incentives, broadband infrastructure investments, digital literacy programs.
Impact Assessment

Benefits: Technological advancements, economic competitiveness, societal transformation.

Challenges: Ethical considerations, regulatory frameworks, digital privacy concerns.

Conclusion

Analyzing major public policies provides critical insights into their design, implementation challenges, and societal impacts across diverse policy domains. By assessing their effectiveness and addressing inherent complexities, policymakers and stakeholders can refine strategies, enhance governance effectiveness, and foster inclusive and sustainable development. As we explore this chapter, understanding the nuances of policy analysis informs evidence-based decision-making, promotes policy innovation, and underscores the imperative of responsive and accountable governance for addressing contemporary societal challenges.

Chapter 27: Examination of Economic and Social Inequalities

This chapter explores the complexities and impacts of economic and social inequalities within societies, examining their causes, manifestations, and consequences across various dimensions.

Economic Inequalities
Income Disparities

Measurement: Disparities in income distribution, wage gaps, and wealth accumulation.

Examples: Wealth concentration among the top percentile, stagnant wages for low-income workers.
Wealth Disparities

Wealth Distribution: Concentration of wealth among a minority, disparities in asset ownership (e.g., property, investments).
Examples: Inheritance disparities, access to financial assets and capital.
Social Inequalities
Education Disparities

Access and Quality: Disparities in educational opportunities, resources, and outcomes.
Examples: Unequal access to quality schools, educational attainment gaps based on socioeconomic status.
Healthcare Disparities

Access and Outcomes: Disparities in healthcare access, quality of care, and health outcomes based on socioeconomic factors.
Examples: Disproportionate health risks, disparities in life expectancy and chronic disease outcomes.
Intersectionality and Multiple Dimensions of Inequality
Gender Inequality

Impact: Disparities in income, employment opportunities, and access to resources based on gender identity.
Examples: Gender pay gap, underrepresentation in leadership roles.
Racial and Ethnic Inequalities

Structural Racism: Systemic barriers and discrimination impacting economic opportunities, education, healthcare, and justice.
Examples: Disparities in criminal justice outcomes, racial wealth gap, disparities in educational attainment.

Causes and Drivers of Inequality
Structural Factors

Economic Systems: Market dynamics, globalization, and technological advancements influencing income distribution.
Examples: Economic policies favoring capital accumulation, deregulation impacting labor rights.
Social Factors

Cultural Norms: Social hierarchies, stereotypes, and discrimination perpetuating inequality.
Examples: Social stigma, biases in hiring practices, access to social networks.
Impacts of Inequality
Social Cohesion

Impact: Strains on social cohesion, trust in institutions, and community resilience.
Examples: Social unrest, polarization in public discourse.
Economic Growth

Effect: Inequality's impact on economic growth, productivity, and long-term prosperity.
Examples: Reduced consumer spending, barriers to entrepreneurship and innovation.
Policy Responses and Interventions
Redistribution Policies

Income Support: Taxation policies, social safety nets, and welfare programs to reduce poverty and inequality.
Examples: Minimum wage laws, progressive taxation, universal basic income trials.
Education and Skills Development

Equality of Opportunity: Investing in education, vocational training, and lifelong learning to enhance social mobility.

Examples: Education reforms, scholarships for disadvantaged students, job training programs.
Conclusion
Examining economic and social inequalities reveals their profound impacts on individuals, communities, and societies at large. By analyzing their causes, consequences, and policy responses, we gain insights into addressing these disparities and promoting a more equitable and inclusive society. As we delve into this chapter, understanding the complexities of inequality informs policy debates, advocacy efforts, and collaborative initiatives aimed at fostering sustainable development and social justice for all.

Policies and Movements Aimed at Promoting Social Justice
Affirmative Action

Objective: Policies promoting equal opportunities and addressing historical discrimination in education, employment, and public contracting.
Examples: Affirmative action programs in higher education admissions, government hiring quotas.
Anti-Discrimination Laws

Legal Framework: Legislation prohibiting discrimination based on race, gender, ethnicity, religion, sexual orientation, or disability.
Examples: Civil Rights Act (1964), Equal Pay Act, Americans with Disabilities Act.
Intersectional Approaches to Social Justice

Intersectionality in Policy

Approach: Considering overlapping identities and experiences (e.g., race, gender, class) in policy formulation and implementation.
Examples: Intersectional feminism in advocacy, inclusive policies for LGBTQ+ communities of color.
Human Rights Framework

Universal Standards: Promoting human rights principles and protections across diverse populations and marginalized groups.
Examples: International human rights treaties, advocacy for indigenous rights, refugee protections.
Environmental Justice
Environmental Equity

Objective: Addressing disproportionate environmental burdens and ensuring fair distribution of environmental benefits.
Examples: Advocacy against environmental racism, equitable access to clean air and water.
Climate Justice

Equitable Solutions: Advocating for policies that address climate change impacts on vulnerable communities and promote climate resilience.
Examples: Indigenous rights in climate policy, global South perspectives on climate finance.
Economic Justice
Income Redistribution

Policy Measures: Taxation policies, minimum wage laws, and social assistance programs to reduce income inequality.
Examples: Progressive taxation systems, earned income tax credits, food assistance programs.

Labor Rights

Worker Protections: Policies safeguarding fair wages, safe working conditions, and collective bargaining rights.
Examples: Fair labor standards, occupational health and safety regulations, unionization rights.
Grassroots Movements and Activism
Social Movements

Mobilization: Grassroots efforts advocating for social justice reforms, raising awareness, and promoting policy change.
Examples: Civil rights movement, Black Lives Matter, #MeToo movement.
Community Organizing

Local Impact: Empowering communities to advocate for their rights, address local inequalities, and influence policy decisions.
Examples: Community development corporations, neighborhood associations, tenant unions.
Global Perspectives on Social Justice
International Cooperation

Global Efforts: Collaborative initiatives addressing global inequalities, promoting sustainable development goals, and human rights.
Examples: United Nations Sustainable Development Goals (SDGs), international aid and development assistance.
Transnational Advocacy

Solidarity Movements: Transnational networks advocating for global justice, human rights, and environmental sustainability.
Examples: Global climate justice movements, solidarity with refugees and migrants.
Conclusion

Policies and movements aimed at promoting social justice play a pivotal role in addressing economic and social inequalities, advancing human rights, and fostering inclusive societies. By examining these initiatives and their impacts, we recognize the importance of collaborative efforts, intersectional approaches, and grassroots activism in shaping equitable policy outcomes and fostering social cohesion. As we explore this chapter further, understanding the diversity of strategies and movements informs advocacy efforts, policy reforms, and global solidarity toward achieving a more just and equitable world for all individuals and communities.

Chapter 28: Global Perspectives and International Relations

This chapter explores the dynamics of global perspectives and international relations, examining key theories, practices, and contemporary issues that shape interactions among nations and global governance.

Globalization: Opportunities and Challenges
Impact of Globalization

Economic Integration: Trends in trade, investment, and technological advancements shaping global economies.
Examples: Global supply chains, outsourcing, digital globalization.
Cultural Exchange

Cultural Influences: Exchange of ideas, values, and cultural practices across borders.
Examples: Global media, migration, international tourism.
Theories of International Relations
Realism

Key Concepts: Focus on state sovereignty, power dynamics, and national interests in international relations.
Examples: Balance of power, military alliances, security dilemmas.
Liberalism

Principles: Emphasis on international cooperation, institutions, and norms to promote peace and cooperation.
Examples: International organizations (UN, WTO), human rights advocacy, diplomatic negotiations.
Constructivism

Social Constructs: Emphasis on ideas, identities, and social norms influencing international relations.
Examples: Identity politics, social movements, norms diffusion.
Global Governance
Multilateralism

Cooperative Frameworks: Collaboration among multiple states and international organizations to address global challenges.
Examples: United Nations, G20, climate agreements.
Global Security

Threats and Responses: Challenges such as terrorism, nuclear proliferation, cybersecurity, and responses through collective security measures.
Examples: International peacekeeping missions, counterterrorism cooperation, arms control treaties.
Global Economic Issues
Trade and Development

Trade Relations: Policies, agreements, and disputes influencing global trade and economic integration.
Examples: Trade agreements (NAFTA, EU), tariffs, trade wars.
Development Goals

Sustainable Development: Efforts to achieve global development goals, reduce poverty, and promote economic prosperity.
Examples: Sustainable Development Goals (SDGs), international aid, global health initiatives.
International Human Rights
Humanitarian Interventions

Protection and Assistance: International responses to humanitarian crises, refugee protection, and human rights violations.
Examples: UN peacekeeping operations, refugee resettlement programs, international criminal tribunals.
Global Justice

Legal Frameworks: International law, human rights treaties, and mechanisms for accountability and justice.
Examples: International Court of Justice (ICJ), International Criminal Court (ICC), Universal Declaration of Human Rights.
Global Environmental Challenges
Climate Change

Environmental Impact: International efforts to mitigate climate change, promote sustainable practices, and adapt to environmental impacts.
Examples: Paris Agreement, global climate summits, carbon reduction targets.
Biodiversity Conservation

Ecological Preservation: Global initiatives to protect biodiversity, wildlife conservation, and sustainable natural resource management.
Examples: Convention on Biological Diversity, wildlife trafficking regulations, marine protected areas.
Conclusion
Global perspectives and international relations encompass a diverse array of issues, theories, and challenges that shape interactions among nations and global governance frameworks. By exploring these dynamics, we gain insights into the complexities of global cooperation, conflict resolution, and collective action toward addressing shared challenges. As we delve into this chapter, understanding global perspectives informs diplomatic strategies, policy formulation, and collaborative efforts aimed at fostering peace, sustainability, and prosperity in an interconnected world.

Chapter 29: Globalization: A Double-Edged Sword

Globalization represents a complex phenomenon with both benefits and challenges, influencing economies, societies, cultures, and governance structures worldwide. This chapter examines the dual aspects of globalization, exploring its opportunities and pitfalls across various dimensions.

Economic Opportunities
Market Integration

Global Trade: Expansion of markets, increased efficiency, and access to diverse consumer bases.
Examples: Global supply chains, multinational corporations, export opportunities.
Investment Flows

Capital Mobility: Investment opportunities, capital access, and economic growth stimulation.
Examples: Foreign direct investment (FDI), venture capital, global financial markets.
Technological Advancements
Information Exchange

Digital Connectivity: Rapid dissemination of information, technological innovations, and digital platforms.
Examples: Internet connectivity, social media, e-commerce.
Innovation and Research

Knowledge Sharing: Collaboration in research, development, and technological advancements.
Examples: Research partnerships, open-source platforms, scientific breakthroughs.
Cultural Exchange
Cultural Diversity

Cross-Cultural Interaction: Exposure to diverse cultures, arts, languages, and global cultural integration.
Examples: Cultural festivals, international cuisine, multicultural societies.
Educational Opportunities

Knowledge Access: Access to global educational resources, international exchange programs, and academic collaborations.
Examples: Study abroad programs, online education platforms, research networks.
Challenges of Globalization
Income Inequality

Disparities: Widening income gaps within and among nations, exacerbating poverty and social exclusion.

Examples: Global wealth concentration, wage disparities, informal economies.
Labor Market Issues

Job Displacement: Dislocation of labor markets, outsourcing, and precarious employment conditions.
Examples: Job losses due to automation, global competition for low-wage labor.
Environmental Impacts
Resource Depletion

Ecological Footprint: Environmental degradation, resource depletion, and climate change impacts.
Examples: Deforestation, carbon emissions, water scarcity.
Global Supply Chains

Environmental Footprint: Carbon-intensive transportation, waste generation, and environmental pollution.
Examples: Pollution from manufacturing processes, plastic waste in oceans, deforestation for agricultural expansion.
Socio-Political Challenges
Cultural Homogenization

Cultural Identity: Threats to local cultures, languages, traditions, and indigenous knowledge systems.
Examples: Cultural assimilation, loss of cultural heritage, cultural imperialism.
Political Sovereignty

National Governance: Challenges to sovereignty, regulatory harmonization, and global governance effectiveness.
Examples: Trade agreements impacting national policies, sovereignty disputes, global governance gaps.
Managing Globalization
Policy Responses

Regulatory Frameworks: Strengthening regulatory frameworks, trade agreements, and international cooperation.
Examples: Environmental treaties, labor standards enforcement, cultural preservation initiatives.
Equitable Development

Inclusive Growth: Promoting equitable development, social protections, and sustainable practices.
Examples: Sustainable Development Goals (SDGs), inclusive economic policies, social safety nets.
Conclusion
Globalization presents a dual reality of economic opportunities and socio-political challenges, influencing diverse aspects of human society and global interactions. By examining its multifaceted impacts, we recognize the importance of balanced approaches, inclusive policies, and global cooperation to harness its benefits while mitigating its adverse effects. As we explore this chapter, understanding the complexities of globalization informs strategic decision-making, fosters international dialogue, and promotes sustainable development in an interconnected world.

Chapter 30: The Impact of Globalization on Politics and Society

Globalization profoundly influences political structures, societal norms, and cultural dynamics worldwide. This chapter delves into the multifaceted impacts of globalization across various dimensions of politics and society.

Political Transformations
Shifts in Power Dynamics

Global Governance: Influence of international organizations, treaties, and global norms on national sovereignty.
Examples: United Nations Security Council, International Monetary Fund (IMF), World Trade Organization (WTO).
Transnational Issues

Policy Challenges: Addressing global issues such as climate change, terrorism, and human rights through collective action.

Examples: Paris Agreement on climate change, UN resolutions on human rights, counterterrorism cooperation.
Economic Integration
Trade and Investment

Economic Interdependence: Integration of economies through trade liberalization, investment flows, and global supply chains.
Examples: Free trade agreements (FTA), regional economic blocs (e.g., European Union), global trade partnerships.
Labor Markets

Global Workforce: Mobility of labor, outsourcing, and impacts on employment patterns and labor rights.
Examples: Offshoring of jobs, migration trends, global labor standards.
Societal Changes
Cultural Exchange

Cultural Homogenization: Adoption of global cultural trends, influence of media, and digital connectivity on cultural identities.
Examples: Globalization of entertainment (e.g., Hollywood movies, K-pop), cultural hybridization.
Social Movements

Global Activism: Transnational advocacy networks, social movements, and civil society initiatives addressing global issues.
Examples: Women's rights movements, environmental activism, global health campaigns.
Technological Advancements
Digital Revolution

Information Access: Connectivity, social media, and digital platforms shaping political discourse and civic engagement.

Examples: Social media revolutions (e.g., Arab Spring), digital diplomacy, online activism.
Technological Innovation

Innovative Solutions: Advancements in healthcare, education, and governance facilitated by technology.
Examples: E-government initiatives, telemedicine, distance learning.
Governance Challenges
Policy Coordination

Global Policy Alignment: Harmonization of regulations, standards, and policies across borders.
Examples: Global health regulations, cybersecurity protocols, international trade agreements.
Democratic Governance

Citizen Participation: Challenges and opportunities for democratic governance in a globalized context.
Examples: E-democracy, participatory budgeting, global governance reforms.
Environmental Impact
Global Environmental Governance

Climate Action: International efforts to address climate change, biodiversity loss, and sustainable development.
Examples: Kyoto Protocol, Convention on Biological Diversity, sustainable development goals (SDGs).
Resource Management

Global Resource Allocation: Challenges of equitable resource distribution and sustainable resource management.
Examples: Water rights, global fisheries management, natural resource conflicts.
Conclusion

Globalization reshapes politics, societies, and global interactions in profound ways, presenting opportunities for economic growth, cultural exchange, and technological advancement, alongside challenges of inequality, governance complexity, and environmental sustainability. By exploring the impact of globalization across these dimensions, we gain insights into navigating global challenges, fostering inclusive development, and promoting cooperation in an increasingly interconnected world. As we conclude this chapter, understanding the transformative power of globalization informs strategic policymaking, international relations, and societal adaptation to build resilient and equitable global communities.

Chapter 31: Benefits and Challenges of a Globalized World

Globalization has brought about significant transformations, offering both opportunities and challenges that shape contemporary societies and global interactions. This chapter explores the multifaceted aspects of a globalized world, highlighting its benefits and addressing the inherent challenges.

Economic Benefits
Market Expansion

Access to Markets: Increased trade opportunities, market access, and economic growth potential.
Examples: Export-driven economies, global market integration, consumer choice diversity.
Technological Advancements

Innovation Acceleration: Rapid advancements in technology, research collaboration, and global knowledge sharing.
Examples: Technological breakthroughs, digital transformation, global R&D networks.
Cultural Exchange
Cultural Diversity

Cultural Hybridization: Exchange of ideas, languages, traditions, and artistic expressions across borders.
Examples: Cultural festivals, multicultural societies, global cuisine diversity.
Educational Opportunities

Knowledge Access: Access to global educational resources, international exchange programs, and collaborative research.
Examples: Study abroad programs, online learning platforms, cross-cultural learning experiences.
Social Progress
Human Rights and Global Advocacy

Global Solidarity: Transnational advocacy networks, human rights movements, and international cooperation.
Examples: Humanitarian aid, refugee protection, global health initiatives.
Healthcare and Public Health

Global Health Initiatives: Collaborative efforts to address global health challenges, pandemics, and disease outbreaks.
Examples: Global vaccination campaigns, disease surveillance networks, international health regulations.
Challenges of Globalization
Income Inequality

Widening Disparities: Global wealth concentration, income gaps, and disparities within and among nations.

Examples: Poverty traps, marginalized communities, global economic divides.
Environmental Sustainability

Ecological Footprint: Environmental degradation, resource depletion, and climate change impacts.
Examples: Carbon emissions, deforestation, loss of biodiversity.
Governance Complexity
Policy Coordination

Global Policy Alignment: Challenges in harmonizing regulations, international treaties, and global governance frameworks.
Examples: Trade agreements, climate accords, international security protocols.
Political Sovereignty

National vs. Global Interests: Balancing national sovereignty with global responsibilities and interests.
Examples: Nationalism vs. globalism debate, sovereignty in international law.
Security and Stability
Global Security Threats

Transnational Challenges: Terrorism, cyber threats, organized crime, and global security cooperation.
Examples: Counterterrorism alliances, cybersecurity protocols, international peacekeeping missions.
Cultural Identity

Cultural Preservation: Challenges to cultural identities, languages, and traditions amidst global cultural homogenization.
Examples: Cultural heritage preservation, indigenous rights advocacy, cultural policy protections.

Managing Globalization
Policy Responses

Inclusive Development: Policies promoting equitable growth, social protections, and sustainable practices.
Examples: Sustainable Development Goals (SDGs), poverty alleviation programs, inclusive economic policies.
International Cooperation

Multilateral Engagement: Strengthening international institutions, diplomatic dialogue, and collaborative frameworks.
Examples: United Nations, G20 summits, regional integration initiatives.
Conclusion
A globalized world presents immense opportunities for economic prosperity, cultural enrichment, and social progress, yet it also poses challenges related to inequality, environmental sustainability, governance complexity, and cultural identity preservation. By exploring the benefits and addressing these challenges, societies can navigate globalization's complexities, foster inclusive development, and promote cooperation toward achieving sustainable and equitable global outcomes. As we conclude this chapter, understanding the dynamics of a globalized world informs strategic decision-making, policy formulation, and global citizenship in an interconnected and interdependent global community.

Chapter 32: International Relations: Diplomacy and Conflict

International relations encompass the complex interactions between nations, characterized by diplomacy, cooperation, and occasional conflict. This chapter explores the fundamental aspects of diplomacy and the dynamics of international conflict, highlighting key theories, practices, and case studies.

Diplomacy: The Art of Negotiation
Diplomatic Practices

Bilateral and Multilateral Diplomacy: Negotiations between two nations or involving multiple states and international organizations.
Examples: Diplomatic missions, embassies, summit meetings.
Soft Power and Diplomatic Influence

Cultural Diplomacy: Promoting national interests through cultural exchange, public diplomacy, and cultural diplomacy.
Examples: Cultural exchanges, international festivals, educational scholarships.
Key Theories in International Relations
Realism

State-centric Approach: Emphasis on power, national interests, and security in international relations.
Examples: Balance of power, military alliances, national sovereignty.
Liberalism

Cooperation and Institutions: Focus on international cooperation, institutions, and norms to promote peace and stability.
Examples: United Nations, international law, economic interdependence.
Constructivism

Social Constructs: Emphasis on ideas, identities, and norms influencing international relations and diplomacy.
Examples: Identity politics, social movements, norms diffusion.
International Conflict: Causes and Resolution
Causes of International Conflict

Political and Territorial Disputes: Conflicts arising from territorial claims, ideological differences, and power struggles.
Examples: Border disputes, ethnic conflicts, geopolitical rivalries.
Conflict Resolution Mechanisms

Diplomatic Negotiations: Peace talks, mediation, and conflict resolution efforts by international organizations and third-party mediators.

Examples: United Nations peacekeeping missions, peace treaties, arbitration.
Case Studies in International Relations
Major International Conflicts

Historical and Contemporary Examples: Analysis of conflicts such as World War I and II, Cold War rivalries, and modern geopolitical conflicts.
Examples: Korean Peninsula tensions, Middle East conflicts, Ukraine crisis.
Diplomatic Successes

Peacebuilding and Mediation: Successful diplomatic efforts in resolving conflicts and promoting regional stability.
Examples: Oslo Accords, Camp David Accords, Good Friday Agreement.
Global Diplomatic Challenges
Emerging Threats

Cybersecurity and Hybrid Warfare: Challenges posed by cyber attacks, disinformation campaigns, and non-traditional security threats.
Examples: Cyber espionage, influence operations, hybrid warfare tactics.
Multilateral Diplomacy

International Cooperation: Challenges and opportunities in multilateral diplomacy, global governance, and collective security.
Examples: UN Security Council resolutions, international sanctions regimes, global health diplomacy.
Future Directions in International Relations
Diplomatic Innovation

Digital Diplomacy: Utilization of digital tools and social media in diplomatic engagement and public diplomacy.

Examples: Digital embassies, virtual summits, online diplomatic exchanges.
Global Leadership

Role of Superpowers and Global Leadership: Influence of major powers, alliances, and coalitions in shaping global diplomacy and international order.
Examples: United States foreign policy, European Union diplomacy, China's Belt and Road Initiative.
Conclusion
International relations are shaped by diplomacy, conflict, and cooperation among nations, reflecting the complexities of global governance, security, and peacebuilding efforts. By examining these dynamics, we gain insights into diplomatic strategies, conflict resolution mechanisms, and the evolving landscape of global relations. As we conclude this chapter, understanding international diplomacy informs global citizenship, fosters diplomatic dialogue, and promotes collaborative efforts toward achieving peace, stability, and sustainable development on a global scale.

Chapter 33: Key Theories and Practices in International Relations

International relations are governed by a framework of theories and practices that shape interactions among states, international organizations, and non-state actors. This chapter explores the foundational theories and practices that define the field of international relations.

Theories of International Relations
Realism

Core Tenets: Emphasis on state-centric behavior, power dynamics, and national interests.
Key Figures: Thucydides, Machiavelli, Morgenthau.
Examples: Balance of power, security dilemmas, sovereignty.
Liberalism

Principles: Focus on cooperation, international institutions, and economic interdependence.
Key Figures: Kant, Wilson, Keohane.

Examples: International organizations (UN, EU), free trade agreements, democratic peace theory.
Constructivism

Concepts: Emphasis on social constructs, identities, and norms influencing international relations.
Key Figures: Wendt, Katzenstein, Checkel.
Examples: Norm diffusion, identity politics, social movements.
Practices in International Relations
Diplomacy

Negotiation and Mediation: Techniques and strategies in diplomatic engagements.
Examples: Bilateral and multilateral diplomacy, summit meetings, peace talks.
International Law

Legal Frameworks: Rules and principles governing state behavior and interactions.
Examples: Treaties, conventions, International Court of Justice (ICJ).
Conflict Resolution

Mechanisms: Processes and strategies to manage and resolve international conflicts.
Examples: Mediation, arbitration, peacekeeping missions.
Contemporary Issues in International Relations
Global Governance

Multilateralism: Challenges and opportunities in global governance and cooperation.
Examples: United Nations, G20, global health governance.
Security Studies

National Security: Strategies and policies addressing traditional and non-traditional security threats.
Examples: Military alliances, cybersecurity, terrorism.
Case Studies and Applications
Cold War

Superpower Rivalry: Analysis of the ideological and strategic rivalry between the United States and the Soviet Union.
Examples: Cuban Missile Crisis, arms race, proxy wars.
Post-Cold War Era

Globalization and Unipolarity: Implications of the post-Cold War world order on international relations.
Examples: End of bipolarity, rise of globalization, humanitarian interventions.
Future Trends and Challenges
Globalization

Impact: How globalization influences state sovereignty, economic policies, and cultural identities.
Examples: Trade liberalization, cultural homogenization, global governance reforms.
Emerging Powers

Shifts in Power: Rise of new powers and their impact on global dynamics.
Examples: China's Belt and Road Initiative, Brazil-Russia-India-China-South Africa (BRICS) cooperation.
Conclusion

Understanding the theories and practices in international relations provides insights into the complexities of global interactions, governance structures, and diplomatic strategies. By examining these frameworks, we gain a deeper understanding of historical contexts, contemporary challenges, and future trends shaping the international system. As we conclude this chapter, recognizing the dynamic nature of international relations informs strategic policymaking, promotes global cooperation, and fosters stability in an interconnected world.

Chapter 34: Case Studies of Major International Conflicts and Alliances

This chapter delves into significant historical and contemporary examples of international conflicts and alliances, analyzing their impact on global relations and diplomatic strategies.

Major International Conflicts
World War I

Causes: Imperial rivalries, militarism, alliances, and nationalism.
Impact: Redrawing of political boundaries, Treaty of Versailles, League of Nations formation.
World War II

Causes: Axis expansionism, totalitarian regimes, and the failure of League of Nations.
Impact: Holocaust, Cold War division, United Nations establishment.
Cold War

Superpower Rivalry: Ideological conflict between the United States and Soviet Union.
Examples: Cuban Missile Crisis, Korean War, Vietnam War, proxy conflicts.
Middle East Conflicts

Arab-Israeli Conflict: Israeli-Palestinian disputes, regional power dynamics.
Examples: Six-Day War, Yom Kippur War, Oslo Accords, Gaza conflicts.
Post-Cold War Conflicts

Balkan Wars: Breakup of Yugoslavia, ethnic cleansing, NATO intervention.
Examples: Bosnian War, Kosovo War, Dayton Agreement.
Major International Alliances
NATO (North Atlantic Treaty Organization)

Formation: Cold War defense alliance against Soviet expansionism.
Evolution: Post-Cold War expansion, role in global security operations.
European Union (EU)

Formation: Economic and political integration of European states.
Impact: Common market, Eurozone, political cooperation, and regional stability.
United Nations (UN)

Formation: Post-World War II international organization for collective security.
Roles: Peacekeeping operations, humanitarian aid, global development goals.
BRICS (Brazil, Russia, India, China, South Africa)

Emerging Powers: Cooperation on economic and geopolitical issues.
Examples: Infrastructure projects, financial cooperation, global governance reform.
ASEAN (Association of Southeast Asian Nations)

Regional Cooperation: Economic integration, political dialogue, and security cooperation.
Examples: ASEAN Free Trade Area, ASEAN Regional Forum, South China Sea disputes.
Conclusion
Case studies of major international conflicts and alliances highlight the complexity of global relations, the impact of historical events on contemporary geopolitics, and the role of diplomatic strategies in mitigating conflicts and fostering cooperation. By examining these examples, we gain insights into the dynamics of international relations, the evolution of alliances, and the challenges of maintaining global peace and stability in a rapidly changing world. Understanding these case studies informs strategic decision-making, diplomatic efforts, and international cooperation efforts aimed at building a more peaceful and prosperous global community.

Chapter 35: Human Rights in the Modern Era

Human rights are fundamental rights and freedoms that every individual is entitled to, irrespective of nationality, ethnicity, religion, or social status. This chapter explores the evolution, challenges, and contemporary issues surrounding human rights in the modern era.

Evolution of Human Rights Concepts
Historical Foundations

Enlightenment Era: Emergence of ideas on individual rights and freedoms.
Examples: Magna Carta, Declaration of the Rights of Man and of the Citizen, Universal Declaration of Human Rights (UDHR).
International Legal Framework

Universal Declaration of Human Rights (1948): Key principles and articles promoting human dignity, equality, and justice.
Examples: International Covenant on Civil and Political Rights (ICCPR), International Covenant on Economic, Social and Cultural Rights (ICESCR), regional human rights conventions.
Contemporary Human Rights Issues
Civil and Political Rights

Freedom of Expression: Press freedom, freedom of assembly, political participation.
Examples: Protection of journalists, advocacy for political prisoners, electoral rights.
Social and Economic Rights

Right to Health: Access to healthcare, sanitation, and disease prevention.
Examples: Healthcare disparities, global health emergencies, access to medicines.
Environmental Rights

Right to a Healthy Environment: Addressing climate change, pollution, and environmental degradation.
Examples: Indigenous land rights, environmental justice movements, sustainable development goals.
Challenges to Human Rights
Violations and Abuses

State-Sponsored Repression: Political repression, arbitrary detention, torture.
Examples: Human rights defenders, freedom of religion, protection of minorities.
Emerging Issues

Digital Rights: Privacy rights, cybersecurity, internet censorship.
Examples: Surveillance technologies, online freedom of expression, digital privacy laws.
Human Rights Advocacy and Movements
Global Advocacy Networks

NGO Initiatives: Human rights organizations, grassroots movements, and advocacy campaigns.
Examples: Amnesty International, Human Rights Watch, global solidarity movements.
Role of International Institutions

United Nations: Human Rights Council, Special Rapporteurs, and mechanisms for monitoring and reporting.
Examples: Human rights treaties, international humanitarian law, humanitarian interventions.
Future Directions in Human Rights
Technological Advancements

Human Rights and Technology: Ethical considerations, artificial intelligence, and human rights impact assessments.
Examples: Digital rights frameworks, technology for human rights monitoring, data protection laws.
Intersectional Rights

Gender and Minority Rights: Intersectional discrimination, gender-based violence, and protections for vulnerable populations.
Examples: LGBTQ+ rights, indigenous rights, disability rights.

Conclusion
Human rights are integral to fostering dignity, equality, and justice globally. By examining the evolution, contemporary issues, challenges, and advocacy efforts surrounding human rights in the modern era, we gain insights into promoting universal human rights principles and addressing global inequalities. As we conclude this chapter, understanding human rights informs ethical decision-making, policy development, and international cooperation aimed at advancing human dignity and ensuring fundamental freedoms for all individuals worldwide.

Chapter 36: The Evolution of Human Rights Concepts

Human rights have evolved significantly over centuries, shaped by historical events, philosophical ideas, and international agreements. This chapter explores the evolution of human rights concepts from antiquity to the modern era, highlighting key milestones and influential figures.

Antiquity to Enlightenment

Ancient Roots

Early Civilizations: Concepts of justice, fairness, and moral codes in Mesopotamia, Egypt, and ancient Greece.
Examples: Code of Hammurabi, Athenian democracy, Stoic philosophy.
Medieval and Renaissance Periods

Feudal Rights: Feudal obligations and rights of vassals, serfs, and nobility.
Renaissance Humanism: Rebirth of classical ideals, emphasis on individual dignity and intellectual freedoms.
Examples: Magna Carta, Renaissance humanist writings, emergence of natural law theories.
Enlightenment and Revolutionary Ideas
Enlightenment Thinkers

John Locke: Natural rights to life, liberty, and property; social contract theory.
Jean-Jacques Rousseau: General will, social equality, and the rights of citizens.
Examples: Locke's "Two Treatises of Government," Rousseau's "The Social Contract."
American and French Revolutions

Declaration of Independence (1776): Assertion of inalienable rights and liberties.
Declaration of the Rights of Man and of the Citizen (1789): Enlightenment principles adopted during the French Revolution.
Examples: Bill of Rights, Constitution of the United States, French Revolutionary documents.
19th and 20th Century Developments
Abolitionism and Civil Rights

Abolitionist Movement: Efforts to end slavery and promote racial equality.
Civil Rights Movements: Struggles for equal rights and freedoms, including women's suffrage.
Examples: Emancipation Proclamation, Seneca Falls Convention, Universal Suffrage movements.
International Human Rights Framework

League of Nations: Early attempts to establish international cooperation and human rights protections.
Universal Declaration of Human Rights (1948): Milestone document affirming fundamental human rights globally.
Examples: Geneva Conventions, International Bill of Human Rights, Human Rights Council.
Contemporary Human Rights Issues
Globalization and Human Rights

Impact of Globalization: Economic, social, and cultural dimensions of human rights.
Challenges: Economic inequalities, environmental degradation, and labor rights.
Examples: Corporate social responsibility, migrant rights, global health disparities.
Emerging Rights Discourses

Digital Rights: Privacy, freedom of expression, and access to information in the digital age.
Environmental Rights: Rights to a clean environment, sustainable development, and climate justice.
Examples: Right to privacy in digital communications, climate litigation, indigenous land rights.
Conclusion

The evolution of human rights concepts reflects humanity's ongoing quest for dignity, equality, and justice. By tracing their historical development from ancient civilizations to contemporary global movements, we understand the foundational principles and challenges of human rights advocacy. As we conclude this chapter, recognizing the dynamic evolution of human rights informs ethical decision-making, policy formulation, and international cooperation in promoting universal human dignity and freedoms worldwide.

Chapter 37: Current Global Human Rights Issues and Efforts

In the contemporary world, human rights continue to be a crucial focal point of international discourse and advocacy. This chapter examines current global human rights issues, highlighting efforts and challenges in advancing human dignity, equality, and justice worldwide.

Key Global Human Rights Issues
Freedom of Expression

Censorship: Restrictions on media, internet freedom, and expression of dissenting views.
Examples: Online censorship laws, suppression of journalists and activists, social media regulations.
Civil and Political Rights

Political Repression: Restrictions on political participation, arbitrary detention, and extrajudicial killings.
Examples: Authoritarian regimes, crackdowns on protests, suppression of political opposition.
Social and Economic Rights

Poverty and Inequality: Access to healthcare, education, housing, and economic opportunities.
Examples: Socioeconomic disparities, lack of basic services, marginalization of vulnerable groups.
Gender and Minority Rights

Women's Rights: Gender-based violence, discrimination in employment, and reproductive rights.

Examples: Gender pay gap, domestic violence, access to education and healthcare.
Minority Rights: Indigenous rights, racial discrimination, and protections for ethnic and religious minorities.
Examples: Minority representation, cultural preservation, land rights.
Environmental Rights

Climate Change: Impact on human rights, environmental degradation, and displacement.
Examples: Climate refugees, environmental justice movements, indigenous land rights.
Global Efforts and Advocacy
International Organizations

United Nations: Human Rights Council, Special Procedures, and mechanisms for monitoring and reporting.
Examples: Universal Periodic Review, Special Rapporteurs, and thematic mandates.
Non-Governmental Organizations (NGOs)

Advocacy Campaigns: Human rights defenders, grassroots movements, and civil society activism.
Examples: Amnesty International, Human Rights Watch, local advocacy groups.
Legal Frameworks and Accountability

International Law: Human rights treaties, conventions, and mechanisms for accountability.
Examples: International Criminal Court (ICC), human rights litigation, and regional human rights courts.
Challenges and Emerging Trends
Technological Advancements

Digital Rights: Privacy concerns, surveillance technologies, and cybersecurity threats.

Examples: Encryption debates, data protection laws, and internet governance.
Global Health and Pandemics

Right to Health: Access to healthcare, pandemic preparedness, and equitable vaccine distribution.
Examples: COVID-19 pandemic response, healthcare inequalities, global health governance.
Future Directions in Human Rights
Intersectional Approaches

Gender and Minority Rights: Intersectional discrimination and protections for vulnerable populations.
Examples: LGBTQ+ rights, disability rights, and migrant rights.
Corporate Social Responsibility

Business and Human Rights: Responsibilities of corporations in respecting human rights.
Examples: Supply chain transparency, labor rights, and environmental sustainability.
Conclusion
Current global human rights issues underscore the ongoing challenges and opportunities in promoting universal human dignity and freedoms. By addressing these issues through international cooperation, advocacy efforts, and legal frameworks, we strive towards a world where human rights are universally respected and protected. As we conclude this chapter, understanding contemporary human rights issues informs ethical decision-making, policy formulation, and collective actions aimed at advancing justice, equality, and human rights for all individuals worldwide.

Chapter 38: Democracy in Action

Democracy stands as a cornerstone of governance worldwide, embodying principles of freedom, equality, and civic participation. This chapter explores the dynamics, challenges, and evolving role of democracy in shaping societies and governance structures globally.

Electoral Politics and Democratic Systems
Electoral Systems

Types: First-past-the-post, proportional representation, mixed systems.
Examples: United States (plurality voting), Germany (mixed-member proportional representation), India (first-past-the-post).
Democratic Governance

Principles: Rule of law, separation of powers, and checks and balances.
Examples: Constitutional democracies, parliamentary systems, presidential systems.
Challenges Facing Modern Democracies
Political Polarization

Divisive Politics: Ideological differences, partisan gridlock, and populism.
Examples: Polarized media, identity politics, erosion of trust in institutions.
Democratic Backsliding

Authoritarianism: Threats to democratic norms, institutions, and civil liberties.
Examples: Erosion of press freedom, electoral manipulation, democratic regression.

Activism and Democratic Engagement
Role of Civil Society

Activism: Grassroots movements, advocacy for social change, and citizen participation.
Examples: Civil rights movements, environmental activism, youth mobilization.
Digital Democracy

Technology: Impact of social media, digital platforms, and online activism.
Examples: Digital campaigns, virtual town halls, e-petitions.
Strategies for Effective Political Engagement
Public Participation

Community Engagement: Town hall meetings, public forums, and civic education.
Examples: Participatory budgeting, citizen assemblies, local governance.
Democratic Institutions

Reform: Strengthening electoral integrity, transparency, and accountability.
Examples: Electoral reforms, campaign finance regulations, anti-corruption measures.
Future of Democracy
Global Trends

Democratic Resilience: Adaptation to technological advancements, demographic shifts, and global challenges.
Examples: Digital democracy innovations, inclusive governance practices, and civic tech solutions.
Democratic Renewal

Citizen Empowerment: Promoting inclusive democracy, civil liberties, and human rights.

Examples: Democratic innovations, civic education initiatives, and international cooperation.

Conclusion

Democracy in action reflects the aspirations of societies worldwide for governance that respects fundamental rights, fosters civic engagement, and promotes inclusive decision-making. By examining the dynamics of electoral politics, challenges facing modern democracies, and strategies for effective political engagement, we understand the evolving landscape of democracy. As we conclude this chapter, embracing democratic values informs participatory governance, strengthens civic institutions, and advances societal progress towards a more just and equitable future.

Chapter 39: Electoral Politics and Democracy

Electoral politics is central to the functioning of democratic societies, serving as a mechanism through which citizens exercise their right to choose representatives and shape public policy. This chapter explores the dynamics, principles, and challenges of electoral politics within the context of democratic governance.

Principles of Electoral Politics
Representation

Electoral Systems: Overview of different electoral systems (e.g., proportional representation, plurality/majority systems). Examples: Comparison of electoral systems in different countries and their implications for representation.
Voting Behavior

Factors Influencing Voting: Ideology, demographics, party affiliation, and strategic considerations.
Examples: Voter turnout trends, swing voters, impact of campaign strategies.
Democratic Processes and Institutions
Election Administration

Electoral Integrity: Ensuring free and fair elections, electoral laws, and regulations.
Examples: Role of electoral commissions, voter registration processes, and monitoring mechanisms.
Political Parties and Campaigns

Party Systems: Multi-party vs. two-party systems, coalition-building, and party competition.
Examples: Campaign finance laws, role of media in elections, and political advertising.
Challenges in Electoral Politics
Political Polarization

Divisive Politics: Ideological divisions, polarization of electorate, and its impact on democratic discourse.
Examples: Partisan gridlock, polarization in media coverage, and electoral outcomes.
Electoral Integrity

Threats to Fair Elections: Voter suppression, electoral fraud, and disinformation campaigns.
Examples: Election security measures, role of international observers, and challenges in digital voting.
Innovations and Reform Efforts
Electoral Reform

Improving Representation: Redistricting, proportional representation reforms, and electoral system updates.
Examples: Ranked-choice voting, electoral reform commissions, and citizen-initiated reforms.
Technological Advances

Digital Democracy: Online voting, e-democracy platforms, and social media in electoral campaigns.
Examples: Use of blockchain technology, cybersecurity in elections, and digital engagement strategies.
Conclusion

Electoral politics plays a pivotal role in shaping democratic governance, ensuring representation, and fostering civic participation. By exploring the principles, processes, challenges, and innovations in electoral politics, we gain insights into the dynamics of democratic societies. As we conclude this chapter, understanding electoral politics informs efforts to strengthen democratic institutions, promote electoral integrity, and uphold the principles of democratic governance worldwide.

Chapter 40: Electoral Systems and Their Functioning

Electoral systems are fundamental to democratic governance, influencing representation, political stability, and the dynamics of political competition. This chapter delves into the various types of electoral systems used globally, their mechanics, and the implications for democratic processes.

Types of Electoral Systems
Plurality/Majority Systems

First-Past-the-Post (FPTP): Candidate with the most votes wins.
Two-Round System (TRS): Runoff election between top candidates if no majority in first round.
Examples: United States (FPTP for most elections), France (TRS for presidential elections).
Proportional Representation (PR) Systems

List PR: Parties present ranked lists, seats allocated based on proportional vote share.
Mixed-Member Proportional (MMP): Combination of PR and FPTP elements.
Examples: Germany (MMP), Netherlands (List PR).
Single Transferable Vote (STV)

Preferential Voting: Voters rank candidates, preferences redistributed until candidates reach a threshold.
Examples: Ireland, Australia (for Senate elections).
Functioning of Electoral Systems
Representation

Fairness: Ability to translate votes into seats proportionally.
Examples: Impact of different systems on minority representation, gender balance in legislatures.
Political Stability

Majority vs. Coalition Governments: Influence on government formation and policy stability.
Examples: Stability in majority-based systems vs. coalition negotiations in PR systems.
Implications for Democratic Processes
Voter Behavior

Strategic Voting: Tactical considerations under different systems (e.g., vote splitting).
Examples: Influence of electoral systems on voter turnout, party strategies.
Party System Dynamics

Party Fragmentation: Impact of electoral rules on party system competitiveness and viability.
Examples: Duopoly in two-party systems vs. multi-party systems under PR.
Challenges and Reform Efforts
Challenges

Gerrymandering: Manipulation of electoral boundaries to favor certain outcomes.
Electoral Fraud: Ensuring integrity and fairness in electoral processes.
Examples: Legal challenges to electoral boundaries, technology's role in preventing fraud.
Reform Efforts

Electoral Reform Commissions: Initiatives to review and recommend changes to electoral systems.

Examples: Public consultations, legislative reforms, and international best practices.

Conclusion

Understanding electoral systems and their functioning is crucial for assessing democratic representation, stability, and fairness. By examining the mechanics, implications, challenges, and reform efforts related to electoral systems, we enhance our understanding of how different systems shape democratic outcomes and governance worldwide. As we conclude this chapter, exploring electoral systems informs efforts to strengthen electoral integrity, promote voter confidence, and uphold democratic principles in diverse political contexts.

Chapter 41: Challenges Facing Modern Democracies

Modern democracies face a myriad of challenges that test the resilience of their institutions, governance structures, and societal cohesion. This chapter explores the key challenges confronting democracies today, analyzing their origins, impacts, and implications for democratic governance.

Political Polarization and Partisan Divides
Ideological Fragmentation

Polarized Politics: Increasing ideological divisions and lack of bipartisan cooperation.
Examples: Gridlock in legislative processes, polarization in media and public discourse.
Populism and Authoritarianism

Rise of Populist Movements: Appeal to discontent with establishment politics, undermining democratic norms.
Examples: Populist leaders challenging democratic institutions, erosion of checks and balances.
Threats to Electoral Integrity
Disinformation and Electoral Manipulation

Social Media Influence: Spread of misinformation, manipulation of public opinion.
Examples: Foreign interference in elections, misinformation campaigns, electoral fraud.
Voter Suppression and Access

Restrictive Voting Laws: Measures limiting access to voting, targeting marginalized groups.
Examples: Voter ID laws, gerrymandering, disenfranchisement of minority voters.
Erosion of Trust in Institutions
Distrust in Government

Public Confidence: Decline in trust in political leaders, institutions, and democratic processes.
Examples: Scandals, corruption perceptions, lack of transparency.
Media Freedom and Press Independence

Threats to Media Freedom: Attacks on journalists, censorship, and media consolidation.
Examples: Press freedom rankings, threats to independent journalism.
Societal and Economic Inequalities
Income Disparities

Economic Inequality: Growing gap between rich and poor, lack of social mobility.
Examples: Wage stagnation, wealth concentration, poverty rates.
Social Fragmentation

Identity Politics: Divisions based on race, ethnicity, religion, and cultural identity.
Examples: Polarization over social issues, rise of identity-based movements.
Technological and Global Challenges
Cybersecurity Threats

Digital Vulnerabilities: Risks to electoral systems, data privacy, and cybersecurity.

Examples: Cyberattacks on electoral infrastructure, online disinformation campaigns.
Globalization and National Sovereignty

Global Interdependence: Balancing national interests with international cooperation and governance.
Examples: Trade disputes, migration pressures, global health crises.
Conclusion
Navigating the challenges facing modern democracies requires robust governance, civic engagement, and safeguarding of democratic principles. By addressing political polarization, electoral integrity, institutional trust, societal inequalities, and global dynamics, democracies can strengthen resilience and ensure inclusive governance. As we conclude this chapter, understanding and addressing these challenges is essential for sustaining democratic values and fostering informed citizen participation in shaping the future of democratic societies.

Chapter 42: Activism and Democratic Engagement

Activism plays a crucial role in democratic societies, serving as a catalyst for social change, policy reform, and civic participation. This chapter explores the diverse forms of activism, their impact on democratic engagement, and the evolving role of activists in shaping political discourse and public policy.

Forms of Activism
Grassroots Movements

Local Initiatives: Community-based efforts for social justice and policy change.
Examples: Neighborhood associations, environmental groups, and youth activism.
Social Movements

Mass Mobilization: Collective action around specific causes or rights campaigns.
Examples: Civil rights movements, feminist movements, LGBTQ+ rights advocacy.
Role of Activists in Democratic Societies
Advocacy and Lobbying

Policy Influence: Lobbying efforts to influence legislative decisions and public policy.

Examples: Advocacy organizations, think tanks, and policy briefings.
Civil Disobedience and Nonviolent Resistance

Protest Movements: Nonviolent protests challenging government policies or societal norms.
Examples: Sit-ins, marches, and demonstrations for civil rights and environmental protection.
Impact on Political Discourse
Shaping Public Opinion

Media Influence: Activists using media platforms to raise awareness and mobilize support.
Examples: Social media campaigns, viral activism, and online petitions.
Policy Reform and Legal Advocacy

Strategic Litigation: Legal challenges to advance civil rights and social justice.
Examples: Landmark court cases, human rights litigation, and constitutional challenges.
Challenges and Opportunities
Institutional Resistance

Government Response: Challenges to activist agendas, crackdowns on dissent, and legal restrictions.
Examples: Surveillance of activists, censorship, and anti-protest laws.
Globalization and Transnational Activism

International Solidarity: Global networks advocating for human rights and environmental protection.
Examples: International advocacy campaigns, solidarity movements, and global protests.
Future Directions in Activism
Digital Activism

Online Platforms: Harnessing social media for advocacy, mobilization, and digital organizing.
Examples: Hashtag campaigns, virtual protests, and online activism tools.
Youth and Next-Generation Activism

Youth Engagement: Empowering young activists, student movements, and youth-led initiatives.
Examples: Youth climate strikes, student activism for educational reforms, and political mobilization.
Conclusion
Activism and democratic engagement are integral to fostering participatory democracy, promoting social justice, and holding governments accountable. By examining the diverse forms of activism, their impact on political discourse, and the evolving strategies of activists, we gain insights into the dynamics of democratic engagement. As we conclude this chapter, recognizing the role of activism informs efforts to strengthen civic participation, protect fundamental rights, and advance inclusive governance in democratic societies worldwide.

Chapter 43: The Role of Citizen Activism in Democratic Societies

Citizen activism is essential to the vitality and accountability of democratic societies, enabling individuals to participate actively in governance, advocate for social change, and uphold democratic values. This chapter explores the multifaceted role of citizen activism, its impact on policy outcomes, and its significance in shaping democratic processes.

Defining Citizen Activism
Citizen Engagement

Active Participation: Involvement of individuals in civic and political affairs.
Examples: Community organizing, grassroots campaigns, and volunteerism.
Advocacy and Mobilization

Campaign Strategies: Tactics for raising awareness and rallying support around specific causes.
Examples: Petitions, rallies, and advocacy campaigns.
Advancing Democratic Values
Accountability and Transparency

Government Oversight: Holding elected officials and institutions accountable.
Examples: Watchdog organizations, public accountability forums, and open government initiatives.
Promoting Social Justice

Equality and Rights: Advocacy for marginalized communities and protection of civil liberties.
Examples: Civil rights movements, LGBTQ+ advocacy, and racial justice initiatives.
Impact on Policy and Governance
Policy Influence

Legislative Advocacy: Influencing policy decisions through lobbying and advocacy efforts.
Examples: Grassroots lobbying, coalition building, and policy briefings.
Community Empowerment

Local Initiatives: Addressing community issues and promoting grassroots solutions.
Examples: Neighborhood associations, environmental stewardship, and urban planning advocacy.
Challenges and Opportunities
Political Resistance

Government Response: Challenges to citizen activism, legal restrictions, and repression.
Examples: Surveillance, censorship, and anti-protest legislation.
Digital Era Activism

Online Platforms: Utilizing social media and digital tools for advocacy and mobilization.
Examples: Digital campaigns, virtual protests, and online petitions.

Future Directions
Technological Innovation

Digital Tools: Harnessing technology for civic engagement, online activism, and data-driven advocacy.
Examples: Civic tech startups, digital democracy platforms, and crowdsourced activism.
Global Solidarity

Transnational Movements: International collaboration on global issues and solidarity movements.
Examples: Global climate strikes, international human rights campaigns, and cross-border advocacy.
Conclusion
Citizen activism is pivotal in safeguarding democratic principles, promoting civic engagement, and driving social change. By exploring its role in advancing democratic values, influencing policy outcomes, and overcoming challenges, we recognize the power of collective action in shaping the future of democratic societies. As we conclude this chapter, understanding and supporting citizen activism strengthens democratic resilience, fosters inclusive governance, and empowers individuals to contribute meaningfully to their communities and beyond.

Chapter 44: Strategies for Effective Political Engagement

Effective political engagement is vital for citizens to participate actively in democratic processes, influence policy decisions, and hold elected officials accountable. This chapter explores strategic approaches and tools for enhancing political engagement, fostering informed citizenship, and promoting civic participation.

Understanding Political Engagement
Civic Education

Knowledge and Awareness: Understanding democratic institutions, rights, and responsibilities.
Examples: Civics curriculum in schools, voter education initiatives, and public information campaigns.
Public Discourse

Civil Discourse: Engaging in respectful dialogue on diverse viewpoints and policy issues.
Examples: Public forums, town hall meetings, and community discussions.
Advocacy and Mobilization
Coalition Building

Collaborative Advocacy: Forming alliances to amplify voices and advocate for shared goals.

Examples: Issue-based coalitions, grassroots networks, and cross-sector partnerships.
Campaign Strategies

Strategic Communication: Crafting messages, mobilizing supporters, and leveraging media channels.
Examples: Grassroots organizing, digital campaigns, and media outreach.
Legislative Advocacy
Lobbying and Advocacy

Policy Influence: Engaging policymakers, drafting legislation, and influencing decision-makers.
Examples: Lobbying efforts, policy briefings, and stakeholder consultations.
Community Organizing

Local Impact: Mobilizing communities around local issues and grassroots solutions.
Examples: Neighborhood associations, community boards, and citizen-led initiatives.
Digital Tools and Technology
Digital Democracy

Online Platforms: Utilizing social media, digital petitions, and e-democracy tools for advocacy.
Examples: Online advocacy campaigns, virtual town halls, and digital engagement platforms.
Data-driven Advocacy

Research and Analysis: Using data to inform policy positions, measure impact, and support advocacy efforts.
Examples: Policy research institutes, data visualization tools, and evidence-based advocacy.
Building Political Capacity
Leadership Development

Training and Empowerment: Developing skills in advocacy, public speaking, and grassroots organizing.
Examples: Leadership programs, campaign schools, and mentorship initiatives.
Strategic Partnerships

Collaborative Governance: Partnering with government, NGOs, and private sector for collective impact.
Examples: Public-private partnerships, inter-sectoral collaborations, and joint advocacy campaigns.
Conclusion
Effective political engagement empowers citizens to contribute meaningfully to democratic processes, shape policy outcomes, and strengthen civic participation. By exploring strategies for advocacy, mobilization, and leveraging digital tools, individuals and communities can enhance their capacity to influence political decision-making and promote inclusive governance. As we conclude this chapter, fostering effective political engagement fosters informed citizenship, strengthens democratic resilience, and advances societal progress towards shared aspirations and collective goals.

Conclusion: The Future of Politics and Society

The future of politics and society stands at a crossroads, shaped by evolving dynamics, global challenges, and the collective aspirations of diverse communities worldwide. This conclusion reflects on the interconnected themes explored throughout this book, offering reflections on the trajectory of democratic governance, societal progress, and the pathways forward for a sustainable future.

Reflections on Interconnected Themes
Democratic Resilience

Adaptability: Navigating political polarization, safeguarding democratic institutions, and fostering civic engagement.
Examples: Strengthening electoral integrity, promoting transparency, and enhancing participatory governance.
Social Justice and Equality

Inclusive Policies: Addressing economic disparities, advancing human rights, and promoting social cohesion.
Examples: Policies for equity, diversity, and inclusion, and initiatives for marginalized communities.
Global Cooperation

Multilateralism: Addressing global challenges through international cooperation, diplomacy, and collective action.
Examples: Climate change agreements, global health initiatives, and conflict resolution efforts.
Predictions and Aspirations for the Future
Technological Advancements

Digital Transformation: Harnessing technology for democratic innovation, digital rights, and cybersecurity.
Examples: Artificial intelligence in governance, blockchain for transparency, and digital inclusion initiatives.
Youth Engagement

Next-Generation Leadership: Empowering youth activism, civic education, and political participation.
Examples: Youth-led movements, educational reforms, and intergenerational dialogue.
Environmental Sustainability

Climate Action: Integrating environmental policies, sustainable development goals, and green governance.
Examples: Renewable energy transitions, conservation efforts, and resilience to environmental challenges.
Call to Action
As we envision the future of politics and society, it is imperative to embrace collective responsibility, democratic values, and inclusive governance. Citizens, policymakers, and global stakeholders must collaborate to address emerging threats, uphold democratic norms, and promote the well-being of all communities.

Conclusion

In conclusion, this exploration of politics and society underscores the complexity, resilience, and transformative potential inherent in democratic governance. By understanding the interconnectedness of political systems, societal dynamics, and global challenges, we can navigate uncertainties, seize opportunities for positive change, and shape a future where democratic ideals thrive and societies flourish. As we embark on this journey together, let us strive for inclusive democracy, equitable progress, and sustainable development for generations to come.

Reflecting

Reflecting on the interconnectedness of the topics explored in this book reveals a tapestry of interwoven themes that underscore the complexity and interdependence of modern politics and society. Throughout these chapters, several key reflections emerge:

Political Systems and Societal Dynamics:
The study of political systems—from democracy to autocracy—demonstrates how governance structures profoundly influence societal behavior and development. Whether examining the evolution of political ideologies or the impact of governmental policies on social equity, each facet highlights the intricate relationship between politics and societal outcomes.

Social Movements and Cultural Influence:

Societal change often emanates from grassroots movements and cultural shifts. Understanding the historical and contemporary contexts of social movements illuminates how activism shapes political discourse and policy agendas. The role of cultural norms and values in shaping political identities and public opinion underscores the reciprocal relationship between culture and politics.

Economics, Policy, and Social Justice:
Economic principles and public policies play pivotal roles in shaping societal well-being and equality. Exploring economic theories alongside policy analysis reveals how decisions on taxation, welfare, and labor rights directly impact social justice outcomes. The examination of inequality and efforts towards promoting equity underscores the imperative of integrating economic policies with social justice frameworks.

Globalization and International Relations:
In an interconnected world, globalization's benefits and challenges are intricately tied to international relations and diplomacy. Case studies of global conflicts and alliances illustrate the complexities of navigating geopolitical landscapes. Discussions on human rights underscore the global responsibility to uphold fundamental freedoms and justice across borders.

Democracy in Action and Civic Engagement:
The vitality of democracy hinges on citizen participation and effective governance. Electoral systems, civic activism, and strategies for political engagement underscore the importance of informed citizenship in sustaining democratic processes. As technologies evolve, digital platforms empower new forms of civic engagement, fostering inclusive and transparent governance practices.

In conclusion, the interconnectedness of these topics underscores the holistic approach needed to address contemporary challenges and opportunities in politics and society. By recognizing these interdependencies, we gain a deeper understanding of how political decisions shape societal outcomes, and conversely, how societal dynamics influence political landscapes. This reflection underscores the ongoing need for collaborative efforts across disciplines and sectors to forge inclusive, resilient, and equitable societies for the future.

In Summary

Predicting the future of global politics and society involves considering current trends, emerging challenges, and aspirational goals for collective progress. Here are some predictions and hopes for the future:

Increased Multilateral Cooperation:
As global challenges like climate change, pandemics, and economic disparities persist, there is a growing recognition of the need for enhanced multilateralism. Countries and international organizations may increasingly collaborate to address these issues collectively, reaffirming the value of diplomacy and global governance frameworks.

Advancements in Technology and Governance:

Technological innovations, including artificial intelligence, blockchain, and big data, are likely to reshape governance structures and democratic processes. There is hope for more transparent, accountable, and participatory governance facilitated by digital tools, enhancing civic engagement and government responsiveness.

Social Justice and Inclusive Development:
There is an ongoing global movement towards achieving greater social justice, equity, and inclusivity. Hopes are pinned on policies and movements that prioritize marginalized communities, reduce inequalities, and promote human rights universally.

Environmental Sustainability:
Addressing climate change and environmental degradation is increasingly urgent. The hope is for more ambitious international agreements, robust environmental policies, and sustainable development practices that safeguard ecosystems and ensure a resilient future for generations to come.

Youth Engagement and Leadership:
Empowering the next generation of leaders and activists is crucial for sustainable progress. There is optimism for increased youth engagement in politics, innovative solutions to global challenges, and a stronger commitment to intergenerational dialogue and cooperation.

Democratic Resilience and Civic Participation:
Strengthening democratic institutions and defending democratic values against authoritarian threats is vital. Hopes lie in bolstering electoral integrity, protecting press freedom, and fostering active citizen participation in shaping democratic processes.

Global Health and Well-being:

Building resilient health systems, enhancing global health security, and ensuring universal access to healthcare are critical aspirations. The COVID-19 pandemic has underscored the interconnectedness of global health and socio-economic stability, emphasizing the need for collective action and solidarity in health crises.

Cultural Diversity and Dialogue:
Promoting cultural diversity, tolerance, and intercultural dialogue is essential for global harmony. As societies become more interconnected, there is hope for greater respect for cultural rights, religious freedoms, and cross-cultural understanding to foster peaceful coexistence.

In summary, the future of global politics and society holds promise for positive transformation through collaborative efforts, technological advancements, and a renewed commitment to democratic principles, social justice, and sustainability. While challenges persist, the collective aspirations for a fairer, more inclusive, and resilient world provide a hopeful vision for generations to come.

Appendices

Appendix A: Glossary of Key Terms

Democracy: A system of government where power is vested in the people, who rule either directly or through elected representatives.

Autocracy: A form of government where absolute power is held by a single individual or a small group.

Political Theory: The study of political ideas, ideologies, and principles that shape political systems and behavior.

Sociology: The study of society, social institutions, and social relationships.

Anthropology: The study of human societies, cultures, and their development.

Globalization: The process of increased interconnectedness and interdependence among countries, economies, and societies.

Public Policy: Government actions, decisions, and programs aimed at addressing societal issues and achieving public goals.

Human Rights: Rights inherent to all human beings, regardless of nationality, ethnicity, or other status, as recognized by international law.

Civic Engagement: Individual and collective actions aimed at addressing public concerns and promoting the quality of community life.

Environmental Sustainability: Practices and policies that ensure the long-term health and viability of natural ecosystems and resources.

This glossary provides definitions essential for understanding the concepts discussed throughout the book, enhancing clarity and comprehension of political and societal topics.

Bonus Chapter: Artificial Intelligence (AI) and Governance

Artificial Intelligence (AI) represents a transformative force with profound implications for governance, decision-making processes, and societal development. This bonus chapter delves into the ethical considerations, policy challenges, and potential benefits of AI integration in governance.

Understanding Artificial Intelligence
Definition and Scope

AI Technologies: Machine learning, natural language processing, and robotics.
Applications: Automation, predictive analytics, and decision support systems.
Ethical Considerations

Algorithmic Bias: Fairness, accountability, and transparency in AI decision-making.

Privacy Concerns: Data protection, surveillance risks, and digital rights.
Policy Challenges
Regulatory Frameworks

Policy Development: Addressing AI deployment, ethical guidelines, and regulatory oversight.
International Standards: Harmonizing regulations across jurisdictions for responsible AI development.
Workforce Displacement

Automation Impact: Job displacement, reskilling initiatives, and labor market disruptions.
Social Equity: Ensuring AI benefits are equitably distributed across society.
Potential Benefits
Enhanced Decision-Making

Data-Driven Insights: Improving policy formulation and resource allocation.
Efficiency Gains: Streamlining bureaucratic processes and service delivery.
Innovative Governance Models

Predictive Governance: Anticipating societal needs and optimizing public services.
Responsive Systems: Real-time data analysis for agile policy responses.
Case Studies and Examples
AI in Healthcare

Medical Diagnosis: AI applications in disease detection and treatment planning.
Public Health: Predictive analytics for disease outbreaks and resource allocation.
Smart Cities

Urban Planning: AI-driven solutions for traffic management and infrastructure optimization.
Environmental Sustainability: AI sensors for pollution monitoring and climate resilience.
Future Directions
Research and Development

Ethics in AI: Investing in research on AI ethics, bias mitigation, and responsible innovation.
Interdisciplinary Collaboration: Engaging stakeholders from technology, policy, and ethics domains.
Public Engagement and Transparency

Citizen Trust: Promoting AI literacy, public consultations, and inclusive decision-making.
Accountability Mechanisms: Establishing frameworks for auditing AI systems and addressing accountability gaps.
Conclusion
Artificial Intelligence presents unprecedented opportunities to enhance governance effectiveness, promote innovation, and address complex societal challenges. However, navigating the ethical implications, policy challenges, and ensuring inclusive benefits require careful consideration and proactive strategies. By fostering dialogue, collaboration, and responsible deployment, AI can contribute to a future where technology supports equitable and sustainable development in governance and beyond.

Bonus Chapter: Disinformation and Misinformation

Disinformation and misinformation pose significant challenges to democratic processes, public discourse, and societal cohesion. This bonus chapter explores the profound impact of fake news, social media manipulation, and information warfare on democratic governance and public opinion.

Understanding Disinformation and Misinformation
Definitions and Characteristics

Disinformation: Deliberately false or misleading information spread with the intent to deceive.
Misinformation: Inaccurate or misleading information spread unintentionally, often due to ignorance or negligence.
Sources and Spread

Social Media: Amplification of false narratives through algorithms, echo chambers, and viral sharing.
Traditional Media: Influence of biased reporting, sensationalism, and clickbait journalism.
Impact on Democratic Processes
Erosion of Trust

Institutions: Undermining trust in government, media, and democratic institutions.
Public Discourse: Polarizing public opinion and fostering distrust among citizens.
Manipulation and Influence Operations

Foreign Interference: Covert campaigns to sway elections, destabilize democracies, and influence policy outcomes.
Domestic Influence: Political campaigns using misinformation to discredit opponents and manipulate voter behavior.
Social and Psychological Effects
Confirmation Bias and Filter Bubbles

Echo Chambers: Reinforcing pre-existing beliefs and isolating individuals from diverse viewpoints.
Psychological Vulnerabilities: Exploiting cognitive biases to manipulate emotions and behaviors.
Public Perception and Behavior

Polarization: Deepening divisions within society based on conflicting narratives and misinformation.
Behavioral Responses: Shaping public attitudes, decisions, and actions through targeted misinformation campaigns.
Countering Disinformation
Media Literacy and Education

Critical Thinking: Teaching skills to evaluate sources, verify information, and detect misinformation.

Digital Literacy: Promoting responsible online behavior and awareness of information manipulation tactics.
Regulatory and Technological Solutions

Transparency: Requiring platforms to disclose algorithms, combat bots, and promote content moderation.
Policy Interventions: Legislation to regulate political advertising, combat fake news, and protect electoral integrity.
Case Studies and Examples
Election Interference

2016 U.S. Presidential Election: Russian disinformation campaigns targeting political divisions and voter suppression.
Brexit Referendum: Misinformation influencing public opinion and voter decisions on the UK's EU membership.
COVID-19 Infodemic

Pandemic Misinformation: Spread of false health information, conspiracy theories, and vaccine hesitancy.
Response Efforts: Fact-checking initiatives, public health campaigns, and social media policies to curb misinformation.
Future Directions
Global Collaboration

International Cooperation: Sharing best practices, intelligence, and regulatory approaches to combat global disinformation threats.
Tech Industry Accountability: Holding platforms accountable for content moderation, algorithm transparency, and user privacy.
Public Engagement and Resilience

Community Outreach: Building resilience against misinformation through community engagement and civic empowerment.

Crisis Preparedness: Developing rapid response strategies and resilience frameworks to mitigate future information crises.
Conclusion
Addressing the challenges posed by disinformation and misinformation requires a multi-faceted approach encompassing education, regulation, technology, and civic engagement. By understanding the impact on democratic processes, public opinion, and societal cohesion, stakeholders can work towards safeguarding the integrity of information ecosystems and promoting informed, resilient democracies in an increasingly digital age.

Bonus Chapter: Climate Change Adaptation and Resilience

Climate change poses unprecedented challenges to global ecosystems, economies, and human societies. This bonus chapter explores strategies for adapting to climate change impacts, building resilience in vulnerable communities, and advancing sustainable development goals.

Understanding Climate Change Impacts
Climate Change Science

Global Warming: Rising temperatures, melting ice caps, and sea level rise.
Extreme Weather Events: Increased frequency of hurricanes, droughts, floods, and wildfires.

Impacts on Vulnerable Communities

Disproportionate Effects: Developing countries, coastal regions, and marginalized communities most at risk.
Loss of Biodiversity: Threats to ecosystems, wildlife habitats, and food security.
Strategies for Adaptation
Resilient Infrastructure

Climate-Proofing: Building infrastructure to withstand extreme weather events and sea level rise.
Green Infrastructure: Using natural systems (wetlands, mangroves) for flood control and coastal protection.
Community-Based Adaptation

Local Knowledge: Incorporating indigenous knowledge and community participation in adaptation planning.
Social Safety Nets: Establishing early warning systems, evacuation plans, and emergency response measures.
Sustainable Development Goals (SDGs)
Integration of Climate Goals

SDG 13 (Climate Action): Mitigating greenhouse gas emissions and promoting resilience to climate impacts.
Synergies with SDG 11 (Sustainable Cities) and SDG 15 (Life on Land): Urban resilience and biodiversity conservation.
Policy and Governance

National Adaptation Plans: Developing strategies, policies, and financing mechanisms for climate resilience.
International Cooperation: Sharing knowledge, technology, and financial resources for global climate adaptation efforts.
Case Studies and Examples
Urban Resilience

New York City, USA: Climate adaptation plans integrating green infrastructure and coastal defenses against storm surges.
Rotterdam, Netherlands: Flood management strategies and innovative water infrastructure to protect low-lying areas.
Rural and Coastal Communities

Bangladesh: Community-based adaptation projects addressing flooding, saline intrusion, and agricultural resilience.
Pacific Islands: Building climate-resilient infrastructure and sustainable livelihoods in the face of rising sea levels and cyclones.
Future Directions
Innovation and Technology

Climate-Smart Agriculture: Adopting drought-resistant crops, precision farming, and agroforestry practices.
Renewable Energy: Transitioning to clean energy sources (solar, wind) to mitigate greenhouse gas emissions.
Education and Capacity Building

Climate Literacy: Educating communities about climate change impacts, adaptation strategies, and sustainable practices.
Skills Development: Training local stakeholders in climate-resilient technologies and disaster preparedness.
Conclusion

Climate change adaptation and resilience are critical imperatives for safeguarding communities, ecosystems, and economies against the impacts of global warming. By implementing adaptive strategies, integrating climate goals into sustainable development agendas, and fostering international cooperation, societies can build resilience and pursue a sustainable future. Efforts must prioritize equity, inclusivity, and community empowerment to ensure that vulnerable populations are supported in adapting to climate challenges effectively.

Bonus Chapter: Global Health Security

Global health security is paramount in safeguarding populations against infectious diseases, pandemics, and other health threats that transcend national borders. This bonus chapter explores the challenges, strategies for pandemic preparedness, and the importance of international cooperation in addressing global health crises, with a focus on lessons learned from events like COVID-19.

Understanding Global Health Threats
Emerging Infectious Diseases

Pandemic Potential: Rapid spread of diseases like COVID-19, SARS, and Ebola across continents.
Zoonotic Origins: Transmission from animals to humans, highlighting the interconnectedness of human and animal health.
Health Inequalities and Vulnerable Populations

Disparities: Unequal access to healthcare, nutrition, and sanitation exacerbating health vulnerabilities.
Humanitarian Crises: Refugee camps, conflict zones, and displaced populations at heightened risk of disease outbreaks.
Pandemic Preparedness Strategies
Early Warning Systems

Surveillance and Monitoring: Tracking disease outbreaks and sharing real-time data to facilitate rapid response.
Global Health Regulations: Compliance with WHO International Health Regulations (IHR) for reporting and response coordination.

Healthcare Infrastructure and Capacity Building

Health Systems Strengthening: Improving healthcare facilities, medical supplies, and workforce readiness.
Training and Education: Equipping healthcare workers with skills for outbreak management and infection control.
International Cooperation and Coordination
Multilateral Institutions and Partnerships

WHO and Global Governance: Coordinating global health responses, setting norms, and mobilizing resources.
Global Fund and Gavi: Funding mechanisms for vaccines, treatments, and health system support in low-income countries.
Public-Private Collaboration

Pharmaceutical Industry: Developing vaccines, antiviral drugs, and diagnostics in partnership with governments and NGOs.
Tech Sector: Utilizing digital technologies for contact tracing, telemedicine, and data analytics during health emergencies.
Case Studies and Examples
COVID-19 Response

Global Vaccine Development: Accelerated research, clinical trials, and equitable distribution of COVID-19 vaccines through COVAX.
Public Health Measures: Lockdowns, social distancing, and mask mandates to mitigate transmission and flatten the curve.
Ebola Outbreaks

West Africa (2014-2016): International aid, community engagement, and healthcare worker training to contain Ebola virus spread.

Democratic Republic of Congo (2018-2020): Vaccination campaigns and rapid response teams to control Ebola outbreaks in conflict-affected areas.
Future Directions
Global Health Diplomacy

Health Security Agendas: Promoting health security as a global priority in diplomatic relations and international policy frameworks.
One Health Approach: Integrating human, animal, and environmental health to prevent future pandemics and zoonotic diseases.
Equitable Access to Healthcare

Universal Health Coverage: Strengthening health systems and ensuring affordable healthcare access for all.
Health Equity: Addressing socio-economic determinants of health disparities and promoting inclusive health policies.
Conclusion
Global health security requires sustained investment, collaboration, and preparedness to mitigate the impact of infectious disease outbreaks and pandemics. By strengthening health systems, enhancing early warning systems, and fostering international cooperation, the global community can better respond to health emergencies and protect the well-being of populations worldwide. The COVID-19 pandemic underscores the urgency of these efforts and the need for a unified approach to build resilient health systems and advance global health security in the face of future challenges.

Bonus Chapter: Technology and Privacy

The rapid advancement of technology presents unprecedented opportunities and challenges in the realm of privacy, data protection, and ethical considerations. This bonus chapter explores the delicate balance between technological advancements and privacy concerns, focusing on regulatory frameworks, ethical implications of surveillance technologies, and strategies to safeguard personal data.

Technological Advancements and Privacy Concerns
Data Collection and Surveillance

Internet of Things (IoT): Proliferation of connected devices and data collection capabilities.
Surveillance Technologies: Facial recognition, biometric data, and location tracking raising privacy concerns.
Big Data and Analytics

Data Mining: Extracting insights from large datasets for commercial and governmental purposes.
Algorithmic Decision-Making: Impact on privacy rights, biases, and transparency in automated systems.
Regulatory Frameworks and Data Protection
General Data Protection Regulation (GDPR)

EU Legislation: Principles for data protection, consent, and individual rights enforcement.

Global Impact: Influence on data privacy laws worldwide and implications for multinational corporations.
National and International Standards

Privacy Laws: Comparing regulations across jurisdictions (e.g., CCPA in California, PDPA in Singapore).
Cross-Border Data Flows: Challenges in data transfer and compliance with international privacy standards.
Ethical Implications of Surveillance Technologies
Mass Surveillance

Government Surveillance Programs: Balancing national security with civil liberties and privacy rights.
Corporate Surveillance: Consumer profiling, behavioral tracking, and implications for user autonomy.
Biometric Data and Privacy Risks

Facial Recognition: Privacy risks, accuracy issues, and concerns over mass surveillance.
Health Data and Genetic Information: Ethical considerations in biometric data usage and privacy protections.
Strategies for Privacy Protection
Privacy by Design

Proactive Approach: Embedding privacy considerations into technology development and implementation.
User Empowerment: Providing tools for data control, transparency, and consent management.
Ethical Guidelines and Responsible AI

AI Ethics: Principles for fairness, accountability, and transparency in AI systems.
Algorithmic Audits: Evaluating algorithms for bias, discrimination, and unintended consequences.
Case Studies and Examples
Cambridge Analytica Scandal

Facebook Data Breach: Misuse of personal data for political profiling and targeted advertising.
Regulatory Responses: Impact on data privacy regulations and public trust in tech companies.
Smart Cities and Surveillance

Urban Surveillance: Implementation of smart city technologies for security and urban management.
Citizen Rights: Balancing public safety with privacy rights in smart city initiatives.
Future Directions
Global Cooperation and Standards

Harmonization of Laws: Collaborative efforts to develop international standards for data protection and privacy rights.
Technology Governance: Multistakeholder dialogues on ethical guidelines, regulatory frameworks, and accountability mechanisms.
Public Awareness and Advocacy

Digital Literacy: Empowering users with knowledge on data privacy risks and rights.
Civil Society Engagement: Advocating for privacy-enhancing technologies and policies that respect individual privacy rights.
Conclusion

The intersection of technology and privacy demands a balanced approach that fosters innovation while protecting individual rights and freedoms. By advancing regulatory frameworks, promoting ethical guidelines, and empowering users with privacy-centric technologies, societies can navigate the complexities of a digital age while safeguarding privacy rights in an increasingly interconnected world. Addressing these challenges requires ongoing collaboration, informed decision-making, and a commitment to upholding privacy as a fundamental human right in the digital era.

Bonus Chapter: Migration and Refugee Policies

Migration and refugee movements are complex socio-political issues that profoundly impact societies, economies, and global politics. This bonus chapter delves into the dynamics of migration, refugee rights, integration policies, and the humanitarian aspects of displacement, examining challenges, policy responses, and human rights considerations.

Understanding Migration and Refugee Movements
Types of Migration

Forced Migration: Refugees fleeing conflict, persecution, and violence.
Economic Migration: Individuals seeking better livelihoods, job opportunities, and economic stability.
Global Trends

Refugee Crisis: Impact of conflicts in regions like Syria, Afghanistan, and South Sudan.
Climate Migration: Displacement due to environmental factors, such as droughts, floods, and rising sea levels.
Refugee Rights and International Law
Legal Frameworks

UN Refugee Convention: Rights and protections for refugees, including asylum seekers and stateless persons.
Humanitarian Principles: Responsibility to protect and assist refugees under international law.
Challenges in Protection

Detention and Rights Violations: Risks of abuse, exploitation, and lack of access to legal representation.
Statelessness: Issues faced by individuals without nationality and barriers to accessing rights and services.
Integration Policies and Socio-Political Dynamics
Host Country Responses

Integration Strategies: Education, employment, healthcare, and cultural adaptation programs for refugees.
Public Perception: Attitudes towards migrants and refugees, xenophobia, and societal integration challenges.
Global Compact on Refugees

UN Framework: Comprehensive response to refugee crises, including burden-sharing, resettlement, and sustainable solutions.
Community Engagement: Engaging local communities in refugee integration efforts and promoting social cohesion.
Humanitarian Aspects of Displacement
Humanitarian Aid and Assistance

UNHCR and NGOs: Providing humanitarian aid, shelter, healthcare, and education for displaced populations.
Emergency Response: Rapid deployment of relief efforts in crisis situations and protracted displacement settings.
Psychosocial Support and Trauma Recovery

Impact on Mental Health: Addressing trauma, stress, and psychosocial well-being of refugees and displaced persons.
Resilience Building: Programs to support coping mechanisms, community solidarity, and cultural preservation.
Case Studies and Examples
European Union Refugee Crisis

Syrian Conflict: Mass displacement, refugee flows, and EU responses to asylum seekers and migration management.
Integration Challenges: Policy debates, societal tensions, and humanitarian assistance efforts in host countries.
Global Refugee Resettlement

Resettlement Programs: US, Canada, Australia, and other countries' efforts in resettling refugees and promoting long-term integration.
Regional Responses: African Union, ASEAN, and other regional bodies' frameworks for refugee protection and regional cooperation.
Future Directions
Protection and Rights

Access to Asylum: Strengthening legal pathways for asylum seekers and refugees, combating human trafficking and exploitation.
Gender and Vulnerable Groups: Addressing specific needs of women, children, LGBT+ individuals, and persons with disabilities in migration policies.
Global Cooperation and Solidarity

Multilateralism: Strengthening partnerships, dialogue, and cooperation among states, international organizations, and civil society.

Development Approaches: Addressing root causes of displacement through conflict prevention, poverty reduction, and sustainable development initiatives.

Conclusion

Addressing migration and refugee challenges requires a comprehensive, rights-based approach that prioritizes humanitarian protection, integration, and global cooperation. By upholding refugee rights, promoting inclusive policies, and fostering community engagement, societies can harness the potential of migration for mutual benefit and contribute to a more equitable and resilient global community. Efforts must continue to uphold human dignity, respect diversity, and build bridges across borders in the face of increasing displacement and global mobility.

Bonus Chapter: Racial Justice and Equity

Racial justice and equity are critical imperatives for addressing systemic racism, promoting social inclusion, and advancing equality in diverse societies. This bonus chapter examines the complexities of systemic racism, the impact of social movements advocating for racial justice, and policies aimed at achieving racial equity and inclusion.

Understanding Systemic Racism
Structural Inequities

Historical Context: Legacy of colonialism, slavery, segregation, and discriminatory practices.

Institutional Racism: Embedded biases in policies, practices, and societal norms perpetuating racial disparities.
Intersectionality

Complex Identities: Overlapping systems of oppression based on race, gender, class, and other identity markers.
Impact on Marginalized Groups: Disproportionate barriers to education, healthcare, employment, and justice.
Social Movements for Racial Justice
Historical Context

Civil Rights Movement: Struggles for racial equality, voting rights, and desegregation in the United States and globally.
Black Lives Matter: Contemporary movement against police brutality, racial profiling, and systemic racism.
Global Impact

Anti-Apartheid Movement: International solidarity against racial segregation and apartheid in South Africa.
Indigenous Rights Movements: Advocacy for land rights, cultural preservation, and self-determination.
Policies and Strategies for Racial Equity
Affirmative Action and Equal Opportunity

Employment Equity: Hiring practices, diversity initiatives, and workplace inclusion policies.
Educational Equity: Access to quality education, addressing racial disparities in academic achievement.
Legal and Justice Reform

Criminal Justice Reform: Addressing racial disparities in policing, sentencing, and incarceration rates.
Restorative Justice: Community-based approaches to healing, reconciliation, and addressing historical injustices.
Community Empowerment and Solidarity
Community-Led Initiatives

Grassroots Organizing: Mobilizing communities for advocacy, policy change, and collective action.
Coalition Building: Building alliances across racial, ethnic, and cultural lines for social justice.
Cultural Representation and Awareness

Media Representation: Diverse narratives, storytelling, and representation in media and cultural industries.
Education and Awareness: Teaching anti-racism, cultural competency, and historical truths in schools and society.
Case Studies and Examples
United States

Civil Rights Legislation: Impact of Civil Rights Act (1964), Voting Rights Act (1965), and Fair Housing Act (1968).
Black Lives Matter Movement: Protests, advocacy for police reform, and policy changes following incidents of racial violence.
Global Perspectives

Truth and Reconciliation Commissions: South Africa, Canada, and other countries' efforts to address historical injustices and promote reconciliation.
European Union: Initiatives combating racism, xenophobia, and promoting diversity and inclusion across member states.
Future Directions
Policy Innovation

Anti-Racism Legislation: Strengthening legal frameworks, accountability measures, and anti-discrimination policies.
Health Equity: Addressing racial disparities in healthcare access, outcomes, and COVID-19 pandemic response.
Educational Reform

Curriculum Diversification: Integrating diverse perspectives, histories, and contributions into educational curricula.
Youth Engagement: Empowering young leaders in advocacy, activism, and promoting social justice.
Conclusion
Achieving racial justice and equity requires collective efforts to dismantle systemic racism, promote inclusive policies, and foster a culture of respect and understanding. By advancing policies that address structural inequities, supporting grassroots movements, and promoting cross-cultural dialogue and solidarity, societies can build a more just, equitable, and inclusive future for all individuals regardless of race, ethnicity, or background. The journey towards racial justice demands ongoing commitment, collaboration, and courage to confront and overcome historical and contemporary forms of discrimination and inequality.

Bonus Chapter: Digital Democracy and Participatory Governance

Digital democracy and participatory governance leverage technology to enhance citizen engagement, transparency, and democratic decision-making processes. This bonus chapter explores innovations in digital platforms, e-participation tools, and online deliberative processes that empower citizens and strengthen democratic institutions.

Evolution of Digital Democracy

Technological Advancements

Internet and Connectivity: Ubiquitous access to information, communication technologies, and social media.
Digital Platforms: Websites, mobile apps, and social networking sites transforming civic engagement and political participation.
E-Participation Tools

Online Consultations: Virtual town halls, surveys, and public forums for gathering public feedback on policies and decisions.
Crowdsourcing: Collaborative platforms for idea generation, problem-solving, and policy co-creation.
Enhancing Citizen Engagement
Direct Democracy

Referendums and Plebiscites: Digital voting systems and online ballots for direct citizen decision-making.
Citizen Initiatives: Online petitions, campaigns, and grassroots movements mobilizing public support for policy change.
Transparency and Accountability

Open Government Data: Accessible information on government activities, budgets, and performance metrics.
Government 2.0: Interactive platforms for monitoring public spending, procurement processes, and regulatory compliance.
Online Deliberative Processes
Virtual Debates and Discussions

Deliberative Polling: Structured forums combining opinion surveys with moderated discussions to foster informed public opinion.

Citizen Juries: Randomly selected panels deliberating on complex issues and providing recommendations to policymakers.
Digital Dialogue Platforms

Online Forums: Real-time debates, Q&A sessions, and expert consultations fostering inclusive dialogue and diverse perspectives.
Social Media Engagement: Hashtag campaigns, live streaming, and interactive content driving public discourse and mobilization.
Case Studies and Examples
Global Initiatives

Open Government Partnership: Multi-stakeholder collaboration promoting transparency, accountability, and civic engagement.
Citizen Assemblies: Ireland's Citizens' Assembly on social issues and constitutional reform through deliberative democracy.
Local Innovations

Smart Cities: Digital platforms for citizen feedback on urban planning, transportation, and community development.
Youth Engagement: Online platforms empowering young people in decision-making processes and civic activism.
Future Directions
Digital Inclusion

Digital Divide: Bridging gaps in access, skills, and participation among diverse socio-economic and demographic groups.
User-Centered Design: Ensuring inclusive and user-friendly digital tools for equitable engagement and representation.
Ethical Considerations

Privacy and Data Security: Safeguarding personal information and ensuring transparency in data collection and usage.
Digital Literacy: Promoting critical thinking, media literacy, and responsible digital citizenship in the digital age.
Conclusion
Digital democracy and participatory governance hold transformative potential in revitalizing democratic processes and empowering citizens in decision-making. By harnessing technological innovations, promoting inclusive participation, and fostering trust in democratic institutions, societies can advance towards more responsive, accountable, and inclusive governance models. The evolution of digital democracy requires ongoing adaptation, innovation, and collaboration to realize its full potential in shaping a more participatory and resilient democratic future.

Bonus Chapter: Economic Inequality and Redistribution

Economic inequality remains a pressing global issue, shaping socio-economic dynamics, political discourse, and policy agendas worldwide. This bonus chapter delves into the complexities of the widening wealth gap, examines policies aimed at addressing income inequality, and explores the profound impact of economic disparities on social cohesion and political stability.

Understanding Economic Inequality
Wealth and Income Disparities

Growth of Inequality: Factors contributing to the concentration of wealth among the top percentile.
Global Perspectives: Disparities across regions, countries, and demographic groups.
Root Causes

Structural Factors: Economic policies, taxation systems, globalization, technological advancements, and labor market dynamics.
Intersections with Social Factors: Race, gender, education, and access to opportunities influencing economic mobility.
Policies to Address Income Inequality
Progressive Taxation

Tax Reform: Redistributive policies, higher tax rates on high-income earners, and wealth taxes.
Social Safety Nets: Welfare programs, unemployment benefits, and social assistance targeting vulnerable populations.
Labor Market Interventions

Living Wage Policies: Ensuring fair compensation, wage floors, and income support for low-wage workers.
Skill Development: Education, vocational training, and job retraining programs to enhance employability and upward mobility.
Impact on Social Cohesion and Political Stability
Social Polarization

Erosion of Trust: Perception of unfairness, disparities in access to opportunities, and social mobility.
Political Fragmentation: Rise of populism, extremism, and polarization in electoral politics.
Policy Responses

Inclusive Growth Strategies: Promoting inclusive economic development, reducing regional disparities, and fostering community resilience.
Democratic Governance: Strengthening institutions, transparency, and accountability to address economic grievances and ensure equitable distribution of resources.
Case Studies and Examples
Global Trends

Post-COVID-19 Recovery: Impact of pandemic-related economic shocks on income inequality and poverty rates.
Developing Countries: Challenges in balancing economic growth with social equity and poverty reduction.
Regional Approaches

European Union: Social cohesion policies, regional development funds, and income support mechanisms.
Latin America: Conditional cash transfer programs, land reform, and policies targeting rural poverty and indigenous communities.
Future Directions

Policy Innovation

Universal Basic Income: Pilot programs, feasibility studies, and debates on unconditional cash transfers.
Green Economy Initiatives: Sustainable development goals, renewable energy investments, and climate adaptation strategies addressing socio-economic disparities.
Global Cooperation

Multilateral Efforts: Coordination among international organizations, development banks, and donor countries to promote equitable growth.
Corporate Responsibility: Corporate governance reforms, ethical business practices, and corporate social responsibility initiatives to mitigate economic inequalities.
Conclusion
Addressing economic inequality requires a multi-faceted approach that combines policy interventions, social investments, and inclusive economic growth strategies. By promoting fair taxation, strengthening social safety nets, and fostering inclusive development, societies can mitigate the adverse effects of income disparities, enhance social cohesion, and ensure political stability. The pursuit of economic equity demands collective commitment, innovative solutions, and sustained efforts to build a more just and prosperous future for all individuals and communities worldwide.

Bonus Chapter: Post-Truth Politics

Post-truth politics has emerged as a significant phenomenon in contemporary political landscapes, challenging the traditional norms of factual accuracy and objective reality in public discourse and policymaking. This bonus chapter explores the dynamics of post-truth politics, the factors contributing to its rise, and its implications for democratic governance and public trust.

Defining Post-Truth Politics
Characteristics

Emotion over Facts: Emphasis on emotional appeals, narratives, and personal beliefs over empirical evidence and factual accuracy.
Misinformation and Disinformation: Spread of false or misleading information through media, social networks, and political rhetoric.
Polarization: Deepening divisions based on ideological beliefs and partisan loyalties.
Historical Context

Media Evolution: Impact of digital media, social networks, and 24-hour news cycles on information dissemination and public opinion.
Political Communication: Shifts in communication strategies, from traditional journalism to digital advocacy and social media campaigns.
Factors Contributing to Post-Truth Politics
Technological Disruption

Social Media Influence: Amplification of echo chambers, filter bubbles, and algorithmic bias in online information consumption.
Digital Manipulation: Spread of fake news, misinformation campaigns, and online disinformation tactics.
Cultural and Societal Shifts

Decline of Trust: Erosion of trust in institutions, experts, and traditional media sources.
Cognitive Biases: Confirmation bias, selective exposure, and motivated reasoning influencing public perception and decision-making.
Implications for Democratic Governance
Policy Decision-Making

Policy Debates: Impact of misinformation on public debates, legislative processes, and policy outcomes.
Public Opinion: Influence of post-truth narratives on voter behavior, electoral outcomes, and democratic legitimacy.
Institutional Challenges

Media Integrity: Role of journalism, fact-checking initiatives, and media literacy in combating misinformation.
Regulatory Responses: Legislative measures, ethical guidelines, and platform accountability to address online misinformation and digital manipulation.
Case Studies and Examples
Global Perspectives

United States: Influence of fake news and social media in electoral campaigns and political polarization.
European Union: Response to disinformation campaigns, electoral integrity, and digital media regulations.
Emerging Trends

COVID-19 Pandemic: Infodemic challenges, vaccine misinformation, and public health communication strategies.
Climate Change Debate: Influence of climate skepticism, misinformation, and public perception on policy responses.
Future Directions
Educational Initiatives

Media Literacy: Curriculum integration, critical thinking skills, and digital citizenship education.
Public Awareness Campaigns: Promoting factual accuracy, responsible information sharing, and ethical communication practices.
Technological Innovations

Algorithmic Transparency: Ethical AI development, algorithmic accountability, and transparency in digital platforms.
Fact-Checking Tools: Automated fact-checking systems, crowdsourced verification, and real-time information verification.
Conclusion
Navigating the challenges of post-truth politics requires concerted efforts to uphold factual accuracy, promote transparency, and safeguard democratic values. By fostering media integrity, enhancing civic education, and fostering informed public discourse, societies can mitigate the influence of misinformation, strengthen democratic governance, and rebuild trust in institutions. The evolution of post-truth politics necessitates adaptive responses, ethical leadership, and collective action to ensure that democratic processes remain resilient, accountable, and responsive to the needs of diverse communities in a rapidly changing digital era.

Bonus Chapter: Artificial Intelligence and Ethics

Artificial Intelligence (AI) is revolutionizing industries and transforming societies worldwide. However, its rapid development raises profound ethical considerations. This bonus chapter explores the ethical implications of AI, including privacy concerns, job displacement, and governance challenges.

Understanding Artificial Intelligence
AI Technologies

Machine Learning: Algorithms, deep learning, and neural networks driving AI advancements.
Automation: Impact on industries, workforce dynamics, and economic productivity.
Ethical Frameworks

Ethical AI Design: Principles of transparency, accountability, fairness, and interpretability.
Bias and Fairness: Addressing algorithmic bias, discrimination, and equitable AI deployment.
Implications for Privacy
Data Privacy
Data Protection: Safeguarding personal information, consent, and data ownership rights.
Surveillance Concerns: AI-powered surveillance technologies, facial recognition, and privacy risks.
Job Displacement and Economic Impact
Labor Market Dynamics
Automation Effects: Job displacement, skills gap, and retraining challenges.

Income Inequality: Economic implications of AI adoption on wages and wealth distribution.
Governance and Regulation
Policy Challenges
Regulatory Frameworks: Balancing innovation with ethical standards and societal impact.
International Cooperation: Global governance of AI, standards, and ethical guidelines.
Case Studies and Examples
Tech Giants
Algorithmic Accountability: Cases of AI misuse, bias detection, and regulatory responses.
Ethical Dilemmas: Autonomous vehicles, healthcare diagnostics, and decision-making algorithms.
Future Directions
Ethical AI Development
Research and Innovation: Responsible AI research, development ethics, and interdisciplinary collaboration.
Public Engagement: Stakeholder consultation, public awareness, and participatory governance.
Conclusion
Navigating the ethical landscape of AI requires proactive measures to ensure technology serves humanity's best interests. By addressing privacy concerns, mitigating job displacement impacts, and establishing robust governance frameworks, societies can harness AI's transformative potential while upholding ethical standards and safeguarding societal values.

Bonus Chapter: Big Data and Surveillance

Big data and surveillance technologies have revolutionized how information is gathered, analyzed, and utilized. This bonus chapter explores the impact of mass surveillance technologies, addresses data privacy concerns, and examines regulatory frameworks aimed at protecting civil liberties in the digital age.

Understanding Big Data and Surveillance
Big Data Technologies

Data Collection: Sources of big data (social media, IoT devices, sensors) and scale of data aggregation.
Analytics: Techniques for processing large datasets, machine learning applications, and predictive analytics.
Surveillance Technologies

Surveillance Methods: CCTV cameras, facial recognition systems, biometric technologies, and satellite imagery.
Digital Surveillance: Monitoring online activities, communications interception, and metadata analysis.
Data Privacy Concerns
Privacy Threats

Personal Data Protection: Risks of data breaches, identity theft, and unauthorized access.
Algorithmic Bias: Impact of biased algorithms on privacy rights and discriminatory practices.
Regulatory Challenges

Legal Frameworks: Privacy laws, data protection regulations (GDPR, CCPA), and jurisdictional challenges.
Surveillance Oversight: Role of oversight bodies, judicial review, and accountability mechanisms.
Impact on Civil Liberties
Civil Rights
Freedom of Speech: Surveillance implications for freedom of expression and online activism.
Right to Privacy: Balancing security measures with individual privacy rights and constitutional protections.
Case Studies and Examples
Global Surveillance Programs

NSA Surveillance: Snowden revelations and implications for global data privacy.
China's Social Credit System: Surveillance state implications on social behavior and individual freedoms.
Corporate Surveillance

Tech Giants: Data collection practices, user consent issues, and corporate responsibility.
Behavioral Advertising: Targeted marketing, consumer profiling, and implications for user privacy.
Regulatory Frameworks and Solutions
Policy Recommendations
Transparency: Public disclosure of surveillance practices and data collection policies.
Data Minimization: Limiting data retention periods and collecting only necessary information.
Future Directions
Ethical Considerations
Surveillance Ethics: Ethical guidelines for surveillance technologies, privacy by design, and ethical AI principles.
Public Discourse: Promoting informed public debate on surveillance practices and their societal impacts.

Conclusion
Navigating the complexities of big data and surveillance requires a balanced approach that protects civil liberties while addressing security concerns. By fostering transparency, strengthening regulatory frameworks, and promoting ethical standards, societies can ensure that surveillance technologies serve public interests while upholding individual rights to privacy and freedom. This chapter encourages readers to critically examine the implications of surveillance in the digital era and advocate for policies that safeguard civil liberties in an increasingly interconnected world.

Bonus Chapter: Environmental Sustainability

Environmental sustainability is a critical global issue, requiring concerted efforts to combat climate change, promote renewable energy, and achieve sustainable development goals. This bonus chapter explores policies, strategies, and innovative solutions aimed at addressing environmental challenges and fostering a sustainable future.

Understanding Environmental Sustainability
Climate Change

Science of Climate Change: Causes, impacts, and projections for global warming.
Climate Action: International agreements (e.g., Paris Agreement), emissions reduction targets, and climate resilience strategies.
Renewable Energy

Transition to Renewable Sources: Solar, wind, hydroelectric, and geothermal energy solutions.
Energy Efficiency: Technologies and policies to improve energy efficiency and reduce carbon footprints.
Policies and Strategies
Promoting Renewable Energy

Government Incentives: Subsidies, tax credits, and feed-in tariffs to promote renewable energy adoption.
Grid Modernization: Smart grids, energy storage solutions, and decentralized energy systems.
Sustainable Development Goals (SDGs)

Agenda 2030: United Nations Sustainable Development Goals, including goals related to clean water, affordable and clean energy, sustainable cities, and climate action.
Integrated Approaches: Addressing interlinkages between environmental, economic, and social dimensions of sustainability.
Innovative Solutions
Circular Economy

Waste Management: Recycling, resource recovery, and waste-to-energy technologies.
Product Lifecycle: Designing products for durability, recyclability, and reduced environmental impact.
Nature-Based Solutions

Conservation: Protecting biodiversity, restoring ecosystems, and enhancing natural carbon sinks.
Green Infrastructure: Urban greening, sustainable agriculture, and resilient infrastructure development.
Case Studies and Examples
Global Initiatives

European Green Deal: Policies for carbon neutrality, sustainable transport, and green innovation.
Global Climate Funds: Financing mechanisms for climate adaptation and mitigation projects in developing countries.
Local and Community Efforts

Community Resilience: Grassroots initiatives, local climate action plans, and community-based adaptation strategies.
Future Directions
Policy Innovation

Carbon Pricing: Market mechanisms, carbon taxes, and cap-and-trade systems to internalize environmental costs.

Climate Finance: Mobilizing investments in green technologies, sustainable infrastructure, and climate-resilient development.
Education and Awareness

Environmental Literacy: Public engagement, education campaigns, and raising awareness on sustainable lifestyles.
Youth Engagement: Empowering youth as agents of change, promoting environmental stewardship and advocacy.
Conclusion
Achieving environmental sustainability requires collaboration across sectors and proactive policy interventions at local, national, and global levels. By embracing renewable energy, advancing climate-resilient infrastructure, and promoting sustainable practices, societies can mitigate climate risks, protect natural resources, and create a resilient future for generations to come. This chapter encourages readers to explore innovative solutions and advocate for policies that prioritize environmental sustainability as a cornerstone of global development.

Bonus Chapter: Healthcare Reform

Healthcare reform is a pressing issue worldwide, focusing on improving access, affordability, equity, and quality of healthcare services. This bonus chapter explores the challenges in healthcare systems, innovations in healthcare delivery, and the shift towards patient-centered care.

Understanding Healthcare Challenges
Access to Healthcare

Health Disparities: Disparities based on socioeconomic status, geography, and demographics.
Barriers to Access: Affordability, insurance coverage gaps, and healthcare provider shortages.
Affordability and Cost Containment

Rising Healthcare Costs: Factors driving cost increases in healthcare services and pharmaceuticals.
Financial Burdens: Out-of-pocket expenses, medical debt, and affordability challenges for vulnerable populations.
Innovations in Healthcare Delivery
Telemedicine and Digital Health

Telehealth Services: Remote consultations, telemonitoring, and virtual healthcare delivery.
Mobile Health (mHealth): Apps, wearables, and digital tools for managing health and wellness.
Integrated Care Models

Care Coordination: Collaborative approaches among healthcare providers, improving continuity of care.

Patient-Centered Medical Homes: Comprehensive, coordinated, and patient-centered primary care models.
Patient-Centered Care
Patient Empowerment

Shared Decision-Making: Involving patients in treatment decisions and care planning.
Health Literacy: Promoting understanding of healthcare information and empowering patients as informed advocates.
Quality Improvement

Outcome-Based Care: Measuring healthcare outcomes, quality metrics, and performance improvement initiatives.
Continuous Learning: Evidence-based practices, clinical guidelines, and continuous professional development for healthcare providers.
Equity and Social Determinants of Health
Addressing Health Inequities
Social Determinants: Impact of socioeconomic factors (education, housing, employment) on health outcomes.
Health Equity Initiatives: Policies and programs to reduce disparities and improve health outcomes for underserved communities.
Case Studies and Examples
Global Healthcare Models

Universal Healthcare: Comparative analysis of healthcare systems in different countries (e.g., single-payer, multi-payer systems).
Innovative Approaches: Successful healthcare reform initiatives addressing access, affordability, and quality improvement.
Local Initiatives

Community Health Centers: Role in providing comprehensive, accessible healthcare services to diverse populations.
Healthcare Innovations: Examples of local programs and initiatives improving healthcare delivery and patient outcomes.
Future Directions
Policy Reform

Healthcare Legislation: Policy recommendations for improving healthcare access, affordability, and equity.
Healthcare Financing: Sustainable funding models, insurance reforms, and payment reforms to support healthcare system sustainability.
Technology and Innovation

Digital Transformation: Harnessing technology for healthcare efficiency, data interoperability, and population health management.
Healthcare Workforce: Training, workforce development, and addressing healthcare workforce shortages and retention challenges.
Conclusion
Achieving comprehensive healthcare reform requires a multifaceted approach that addresses systemic challenges while embracing innovations in healthcare delivery and promoting patient-centered care. By prioritizing healthcare access, affordability, equity, and quality improvement, societies can foster healthier communities and ensure healthcare systems meet the needs of all individuals. This chapter encourages readers to advocate for healthcare reform initiatives that prioritize patient well-being and promote sustainable healthcare practices in an evolving global landscape.

Bonus Chapter: Global Trade and Economic Integration

Global trade and economic integration are fundamental drivers of national economies and global prosperity. This bonus chapter explores the effects of trade agreements, economic globalization, and protectionism on global economies, industries, and international relations.

Understanding Global Trade Dynamics
Trade Agreements

Free Trade Agreements (FTAs): Benefits, challenges, and economic implications for participating countries.
Regional Trade Blocs: EU, NAFTA/USMCA, ASEAN, Mercosur, and their impact on regional economic integration.
Globalization and Economic Interdependence

Supply Chains: Global production networks, outsourcing, and the interconnectedness of global economies.
Trade Liberalization: Tariff reductions, trade barriers, and fostering global competitiveness.
Economic Impacts and Benefits
Prosperity and Growth

GDP Growth: Impact of international trade on national economic growth and development.
Job Creation: Employment opportunities, labor market dynamics, and income distribution effects.
Industry Specific Effects

Sectoral Impact: Agriculture, manufacturing, services, and technological innovation driven by global trade.
Emerging Markets: Opportunities and challenges for developing countries in global trade networks.
Challenges and Controversies
Protectionism

Trade Barriers: Tariffs, quotas, and non-tariff barriers to trade (e.g., subsidies, import restrictions).
Trade Wars: Economic implications of trade disputes and retaliatory measures among trading partners.
Global Economic Governance

Multilateral Institutions: WTO, IMF, World Bank, and their role in shaping global trade rules and policies.
Trade Negotiations: Challenges in reaching consensus on trade agreements and addressing trade imbalances.
Case Studies and Examples
Bilateral Trade Relationships

US-China Trade Relations: Impact of tariffs, trade deficits, and geopolitical tensions on global markets.
EU-UK Trade Relations: Brexit implications, trade negotiations, and economic consequences for Europe and the UK.
Trade and Development

Africa and Global Trade: Role of trade in economic development, infrastructure investment, and poverty reduction.
Asia-Pacific Trade Dynamics: Regional integration efforts, trade corridors, and economic growth prospects.
Future Directions
Global Trade Policy

Trade Reform: Modernizing trade agreements, addressing digital trade, and intellectual property rights.
Sustainable Development Goals: Integrating trade policies with environmental sustainability and social equity goals.
Adapting to Global Challenges

Resilience Strategies: Building economic resilience to external shocks, pandemics, and climate change impacts.
Inclusive Growth: Promoting fair trade practices, addressing income inequality, and fostering inclusive economic development.
Conclusion
Global trade and economic integration play a pivotal role in shaping national economies and global prosperity. By understanding the complexities of trade agreements, economic globalization, and the impact of protectionism, societies can navigate challenges and harness opportunities for sustainable economic growth and development. This chapter encourages readers to advocate for policies that promote open and fair trade practices while addressing global economic disparities in an interconnected world.

Bonus Chapter: Cybersecurity and National Security

Cybersecurity is paramount in safeguarding national security, protecting critical infrastructure, and balancing security measures with civil liberties. This bonus chapter explores the evolving threats posed by cyberattacks, strategies for securing critical infrastructure, and ethical considerations in cybersecurity policies.

Understanding Cybersecurity Threats
Cyber Threat Landscape

Types of Cyberattacks: Malware, ransomware, phishing, and advanced persistent threats (APTs).
State-Sponsored Attacks: Cyber espionage, disinformation campaigns, and geopolitical implications.
Vulnerabilities and Risks

Critical Infrastructure: Energy, telecommunications, finance, healthcare, and transportation sectors.
Supply Chain Risks: Third-party vendors, software vulnerabilities, and supply chain attacks.
Strategies for Securing Critical Infrastructure
Defense Mechanisms

Cyber Defense Strategies: Incident response plans, threat intelligence, and cybersecurity frameworks (e.g., NIST, ISO).

Encryption and Data Protection: Securing sensitive information and mitigating data breaches.
Public-Private Partnerships

Collaborative Efforts: Information sharing, sector-specific cybersecurity initiatives, and public-private cooperation.
Regulatory Measures: Compliance requirements, cybersecurity standards, and regulatory oversight.
Balancing Security and Civil Liberties
Privacy Concerns

Surveillance Technologies: Monitoring capabilities, privacy implications, and legal safeguards.
Data Privacy Laws: Protection of personal data, transparency, and individual rights in cyberspace.
Ethical Considerations

Ethical Use of Cyber Tools: Cyber deterrence, offensive cyber operations, and international norms.
Human Rights: Balancing security imperatives with freedom of expression, privacy rights, and civil liberties.
Case Studies and Examples
Major Cyber Incidents

Critical Infrastructure Attacks: Examples of cyberattacks targeting energy grids, financial systems, and healthcare facilities.
State-Sponsored Cyber Operations: Case studies of cyber espionage, election interference, and geopolitical tensions.
Resilience and Response

Cyber Resilience: Building adaptive capabilities, continuity planning, and rapid response to cyber incidents.
International Cooperation: Cybersecurity cooperation, diplomatic efforts, and global response frameworks (e.g., Budapest Convention).

Future Directions
Emerging Technologies

AI and Machine Learning: Applications in cybersecurity, threat detection, and autonomous defense systems.
Quantum Computing: Implications for encryption, cybersecurity defenses, and future cyber threats.
Policy and Governance

Cybersecurity Legislation: Strengthening cyber defenses, promoting cybersecurity research, and fostering international cyber norms.
Capacity Building: Cyber workforce development, education initiatives, and building cyber resilience across sectors.
Conclusion
Cybersecurity is critical to national security, economic stability, and protecting civil liberties in the digital age. By understanding cyber threats, implementing robust defense strategies, and promoting responsible cyber behavior, societies can mitigate risks and build resilient cybersecurity frameworks. This chapter encourages readers to advocate for policies that strike a balance between security imperatives and safeguarding individual freedoms in an interconnected and technologically-driven world.

Bonus Chapter: Gender Equality and Women's Rights

Gender equality and women's rights are fundamental principles for achieving social justice, economic development, and sustainable peace. This bonus chapter explores advocacy for gender parity in leadership, addressing gender-based violence, and promoting equal opportunities in education and employment.

Understanding Gender Equality Issues
Gender Parity in Leadership

Representation: Challenges and progress in achieving equal representation of women in leadership roles.
Political Empowerment: Strategies for increasing women's participation in political decision-making and governance.
Addressing Gender-Based Violence

Forms of Violence: Domestic violence, sexual harassment, human trafficking, and harmful traditional practices.
Legal Protections: Legislation, policies, and international frameworks addressing gender-based violence.
Promoting Equal Opportunities
Education and Skills Development

Access to Education: Barriers to girls' education, promoting STEM education for girls, and vocational training opportunities.
Career Advancement: Breaking barriers to women's advancement in traditionally male-dominated fields and leadership positions.
Workplace Equality

Equal Pay: Closing the gender pay gap, pay transparency, and promoting fair compensation policies.
Work-Life Balance: Policies supporting parental leave, childcare facilities, and flexible work arrangements.
Advocacy and Social Change
Social Movements

Feminist Movements: Historical perspectives, contemporary advocacy, and intersectionality in feminist activism.
Youth Engagement: Empowering young women as advocates for gender equality and social justice.
Legal and Policy Frameworks

Human Rights Framework: International human rights treaties and conventions promoting gender equality and women's rights.
Gender Mainstreaming: Integrating gender perspectives into policies, programs, and development initiatives.
Case Studies and Examples
Global Initiatives

UN Sustainable Development Goals: Goal 5 (Gender Equality) and efforts to achieve gender parity in all sectors.
Corporate Leadership: Best practices in promoting gender diversity on corporate boards and leadership teams.
Local and Community Efforts

Community-Led Initiatives: Grassroots efforts, community partnerships, and local governance promoting gender equality.

Impact of COVID-19: Gender disparities exacerbated by the pandemic and resilience strategies for women and girls.

Future Directions

Policy Reform

Legal Reforms: Strengthening laws against gender discrimination, gender-based violence, and ensuring legal protections.

Inclusive Policies: Gender-responsive budgeting, healthcare access, and social protection measures.

Education and Awareness

Gender Sensitization: Education campaigns, training programs, and promoting gender-responsive teaching practices.

Media and Communication: Role of media in shaping gender norms, promoting positive representations, and countering stereotypes.

Conclusion

Achieving gender equality and advancing women's rights requires collective action, advocacy, and policy reforms at local, national, and global levels. By addressing gender disparities, promoting women's leadership, and combating gender-based violence, societies can create inclusive environments where all individuals can thrive. This chapter encourages readers to advocate for gender equality, support women's empowerment initiatives, and contribute to building a more equitable and just world for future generations.

Bonus Chapter: Education Reform

Education reform is essential for meeting the evolving needs of students in the 21st century. This bonus chapter explores innovations in educational technology, curriculum development, and strategies for addressing disparities in access to quality education.

Innovations in Educational Technology
Digital Learning Platforms

Online Learning: Benefits of digital platforms for remote education, accessibility, and personalized learning experiences.
EdTech Tools: Interactive simulations, virtual reality (VR), and augmented reality (AR) in education.
Blended Learning Models

Hybrid Classrooms: Integration of online and traditional classroom instruction, fostering student engagement and collaboration.
Flipped Classroom: Reversing traditional teaching methods, promoting active learning and critical thinking skills.
Curriculum Development and Educational Practices

STEM Education

Promoting STEM: Initiatives to enhance STEM (Science, Technology, Engineering, Mathematics) education, encouraging diversity and inclusivity.
Project-Based Learning: Real-world applications, problem-solving skills, and interdisciplinary approaches.
Social and Emotional Learning (SEL)

Emotional Intelligence: Developing empathy, resilience, and social skills in students.
Inclusive Education: Addressing diversity, equity, and cultural responsiveness in curriculum development and classroom practices.
Addressing Disparities in Access to Education
Digital Divide

Access to Technology: Bridging the digital divide, providing internet access, and affordable devices to underserved communities.
Rural and Remote Education: Challenges and innovative solutions for delivering quality education in rural areas.
Equity in Education

Closing Achievement Gaps: Strategies to support disadvantaged students, reduce dropout rates, and promote academic success.
Teacher Training: Professional development, cultural competence, and inclusive teaching practices.
Case Studies and Examples
Global Initiatives

UNESCO Education 2030 Agenda: Goals for inclusive and equitable quality education and lifelong learning opportunities.

Innovative Schools: Examples of schools and educational institutions implementing transformative practices and achieving positive outcomes.
Technology Integration

Emerging Trends: AI in education, adaptive learning technologies, and data-driven insights for personalized learning.
Education Policy Reforms: Policy initiatives supporting educational innovation and improving learning outcomes.
Future Directions
Policy and Governance

Education Policy Reforms: Legislative frameworks, funding initiatives, and public-private partnerships to support educational innovation.
Global Collaboration: International cooperation, knowledge sharing, and best practices in education reform.
Digital Literacy

21st-Century Skills: Critical thinking, digital literacy, and preparing students for future careers in a rapidly evolving global economy.
Educational Equity: Advocacy for equal access to quality education as a fundamental human right.
Conclusion
Education reform is vital for preparing students to succeed in a globalized, technology-driven world. By embracing innovative practices, addressing disparities in access, and fostering inclusive learning environments, societies can empower future generations to thrive and contribute to a sustainable future. This chapter encourages readers to support education reform initiatives that prioritize equity, innovation, and lifelong learning opportunities for all.

Bonus Chapter: Urbanization and Smart Cities

Urbanization presents opportunities and challenges for sustainable development and quality of life in cities worldwide. This bonus chapter explores the benefits of urban growth, challenges of sustainable urban planning, and leveraging technology for smarter, more resilient cities.

Benefits and Challenges of Urban Growth
Economic Opportunities

Urbanization Trends: Population growth, urban economies, and attracting investments in urban areas.
Job Creation: Employment opportunities, economic diversification, and fostering innovation hubs.
Environmental Sustainability

Green Urban Planning: Sustainable development goals, reducing carbon footprint, and promoting eco-friendly infrastructure.
Urban Resilience: Climate change adaptation, disaster preparedness, and building resilient communities.

Sustainable Urban Planning
Smart Cities Concept

Digital Infrastructure: IoT (Internet of Things), sensors, and data analytics for optimizing city operations and services.
Smart Mobility: Public transportation systems, reducing traffic congestion, and promoting sustainable transportation options.
Community Engagement

Urban Governance: Citizen participation, transparency in decision-making, and promoting inclusive urban policies.
Public Spaces: Parks, green spaces, and cultural amenities enhancing quality of life and social cohesion.
Leveraging Technology for Smarter Cities
Digital Transformation

Urban Data Analytics: Big data insights, predictive modeling, and enhancing urban planning and decision-making.
Energy Efficiency: Smart grids, renewable energy integration, and promoting energy-efficient buildings.
Inclusive and Accessible Cities

Digital Inclusion: Bridging the digital divide, ensuring equitable access to digital services and information.
Age-Friendly Cities: Designing cities for all ages, promoting accessibility, and enhancing quality of life for senior citizens.
Case Studies and Examples
Global City Initiatives

Smart City Projects: Examples of successful smart city initiatives and lessons learned from global cities.
Urban Innovations: Sustainable urban regeneration, adaptive reuse of spaces, and revitalizing urban communities.
Local Solutions

Community-Led Initiatives: Grassroots efforts, participatory urban planning, and fostering resilient neighborhoods.
Urban Renewal: Revitalization projects, heritage conservation, and preserving cultural identity in urban landscapes.
Future Directions
Policy and Governance

Urban Policy Reforms: Integrated urban planning, zoning regulations, and promoting sustainable urban development goals.
Technology Integration: AI, blockchain, and smart technologies advancing urban innovation and resilience.
Resilient Cities

Climate Adaptation: Building climate-resilient infrastructure, green building standards, and reducing urban vulnerabilities.
Global Collaboration: International partnerships, knowledge exchange, and best practices for sustainable urbanization.
Conclusion
Urbanization and smart cities present unprecedented opportunities for economic growth, innovation, and improving quality of life. By embracing sustainable urban planning, leveraging technology, and fostering inclusive communities, cities can become engines of prosperity and resilience in a rapidly urbanizing world. This chapter encourages readers to support policies and initiatives that promote sustainable urban development and enhance urban resilience for future generations.